MY TRIP ABROAD

Europe in 1936

Frank J. Daily

5837 S. Union Avenue
Chicago, Illinois
Telephone: Normal 5625

My Trip Abroad: Europe in 1936

©2017 Frank Daily

First printing

ISBN-13: 978-1544640204

Front cover: *The T.S.S. Statendam,* public domain image.
Back cover: Frank J. Daily
Photos on pages 80, 83, 113, and 130 are courtesy of the Library of Congress.
Photos on pages 36, 55, and 67 are courtesy of Wikipedia Commons.
Photo on page 115 (top) is courtesy Bains News Service.
All other images are public domain.

For more information contact:
Frank Daily
4614 N. Lake Drive
Whitefish Bay, Wisconsin 53211

Table of Contents

The cover of Frank J. Daily's journal

Prologue

In the summer of 1936, as the country was slowly crawling out of the Great Depression and a record breaking heat wave was descending upon Chicago and the rest of the country, a 30-year-old bachelor public school teacher, who still lived at home, set out to fulfill his dreams on what for him was "The Trip of a Lifetime."

Through his friendship with a travel agent named William Beale, my father, Frank Daily, who I was named after, was able to secure passage on a cruise ship as part of a two-month tour of much of Western Europe. William Beale, referred to variously as "Bill" and "W.B.", was the travel agent who organized and led this tour. I do not know how my father got to know him or arranged to travel with him—let alone afford such luxury. The ebullient Mr. Beale remained a friend of my father for a few years during my early childhood, but I have no recollection of what became of him. My father had dreamed of making such a trip since boyhood, growing up on the South Side of Chicago as the second youngest of nine children of Francis and Wilhelmena "Minnie" (Webber) Daily and the only one of his siblings to graduate from high school or college.

He left a journal of his travels, which I found and kept after his death. Much of it was very difficult to read because of handwriting and ink that had faded over the decades since he had written and recorded his observations, but I believe I have accurately replicated it during many hours of reviewing, reading, editing and revising the drafts I prepared.

I found the level of his vocabulary, appreciation of culture and eye for detail remarkable in every way—especially given the humble and modest circumstances of his childhood home and surroundings. His teaching colleagues referred to him as "Dictionary Daily" because of his expansive vocabulary, which he enjoyed using—a distinction that always gave him great pleasure.

His extraordinary eloquence is on full display in the journal he kept, at times sending me to the dictionary to determine the meaning of a descriptive word.

Inspired by the legacy of his curiosity and appreciation of culture, history and European travel, my wife Julie Ebert and I have traveled to many of the places described in his journal—places like London (1995), Milan (2000), Rome (2000 and 2007), Brussels (2001), Paris and Versailles (2004), Munich, Wiesbaden and Frankfurt (2009), Amsterdam (2008 and 2009), and Cologne (2016). In each place we were amazed by the accuracy and detail of his descriptions, as viewed many decades later.

Some portions of the journal did not have complete sentences. There also were gaps, and even I recognize only a very few of the names mentioned such as: William Beale, William Dempsy (my godfather), Mary Murphy (my godmother), Ida Burke (my aunt who married my uncle Harold Daily long after the time of her mention here) and Joe Pandalfo, a long-time family friend from Chicago.

My goal was to reproduce the journal virtually verbatim to capture fully the uniquely thorough and creative story it recounts. And with it, an appreciation of what life was like for an American traveling in Europe 80 years ago. From time to time I have added editorial notes and comments to clarify, or expand on the passage as he had written it originally. They will be labeled as *[Editor's Notes.]*

Come now and travel with my father back in time and place as he explores Europe in 1936.

—*Frank Daily*
Milwaukee, Wisconsin
December 2016

CHAPTER 1

Bon Voyage—the adventure begins

June 11, 1936
Place: Chicago and departure to New York
Weather: Cool

Much hesitation over substituting bus for train. Considerations: save money, which could be used advantageously at European capitals; sufficient time; new experience and long trip. After lunch with comfortable companions, George McGonigle and Bud Kenney, at Younkers (during which we commented upon the physique of the manageress), Bud took me to the bus station. True to my original reactions thereto, the terminal seemed to me a miniature Ellis Island in regards to the type of people and the attitude toward them. Most people seemed to take the bus because they could afford no other mode of transportation. Three incidents made me forget, temporarily, my dislike of bus travel. They were: 1) the delivery of a mysterious package, which was found to contain a book, George Santayana's "The Last Puritan," the unexpected and wholly welcome gift of Mae Reidy and Virginia Berry; 2) the description of the bus as "THE LUXURY LIMITED" (giving rise to the hope that the title might represent something different from the usual); and 3) on the arrival of the bus, being given the choice front seat arranged for me by William Beale.

Once on the bus I resolved to make the best of things, although with the heavy traffic and stops in Gary and other places, I almost despaired.

When finally we struck the open road, the desire to and necessity of conserving one's energy became quite real. Even to carry on a desultory conversation with my seat companion, an Oak Park High School boy, seemed to sap my energy.

We roared along the road at 53 mph (the bus has a governor affixed, which prevents it from going faster—a fact which apparently is not generally known).

The prime consideration seems to be comfort at all cost. I was much impressed with the superior driving skills and the clean, natty attire of the various drivers. Though the passengers look like a tired, mussed mob of uncomfortables, the drivers, even after eight hours of work, looked fresh and unaffected.

About every two hours we stopped for 10 or 15 minutes of rest and refreshments. It is surprising the amount of food the passengers have eaten. That is because the next stop, though only two hours away, seems to follow only after much jolting and languishing in the seat.

The more extended the trip the more acute the inconveniences. Food is taken only because it represents a memory of more comfortable occasions.

Attractions announced by the driver received little or no attention from the riders. They turn their heads listlessly in the direction of the attraction for a moment and immediately return to head rolling in an effort to obtain some position of comfort.

Cleveland, which we reached the evening of Kansas Gov. Alf Landon's nomination during the Republican National Convention, was merely a brightly lighted city filled with silly yelling people, roaring nonsensically. From there a darkened bus roared through the night carrying its stiff-jointed, heavy lidded sleepless sufferers.

There is a peculiar feeling of stiffness and unfamiliarity among the passengers, which quickly dissipates when the inability of certain passengers to follow regulations becomes evident. Anything obvious calls for frequent remarks and chuckles over their discomfiture.

When seemingly endless Pennsylvania is being crossed, we see the last vestiges of the record flood of last spring. Huge piles of debris, containing trees, parts of bridges, auto tires and other rubbish lay as dirty brownish messes at intervals along the bank. Some are buildings, their foundations swept away, rested as shattered crates, some upright but split in sections, others turned partly or entirely over. Trees near the banks are still warped and turned as if being in a raging hurricane.

[Editor's Note: The reference here is to Johnstown, Pennsylvania's second disastrous flood, which struck on March 17, 1936, causing property loss of $50 million—far greater than the damages incurred in the original catastrophic flood of May 31, 1889. Evidence of the fury unleashed by raging flood waters, as it still existed three months later, is eloquently recorded and described here.]

Arriving in New York at 5:30 p.m., we succeeded in encountering what seemed to be every single car in New York State within the city. A fast, dizzy trip through the roaring Holland Tunnel, with its white enameled brick interior, brought us in a state of delirious fatigue to our destination.

From there we traveled in a bumpy cab ride to the Wellington Hotel where the presence of William Beale assured me I was not dreaming. We then went to dinner at the Taft Hotel, and then back to the Wellington and off with a rowdy cabbie carrying us through a noisy railroad district to the Hoboken Ferry, which transported us across the river, without my knowing we had even moved. Fare: example of racket—$1.25 apiece, the meter registered $1.50 total. No one, including the hotels, seemed to be able to do anything about it.

Pulling up to the dock I sighted a large steamer with white stacks painted with green and yellow stripes. No difficulty entering the sheds. Walking up the gangplank, I called to mind my impressions of the feeling people might have as represented in the movies. No reaction—just a desire to leave the bags in my stateroom and walk around the ship. Impressions as to size and furnishings: unfavorable. Concluded however that the current rage for large luxury liners formed prejudice against others. Much partying aboard boat. Attendants are typical seamen, on duty and helpful. Much calling out for wires, and letters for passengers. Gangplank up—decision of any to go back, too late. Crowd on wharf starts cheering and yelling advice. Much waving, little crying.

Everyone remains at the rails to see the New York skyline, and the Statue of Liberty. Leave New York view and settle down to walk about and sound out possible comfortable companions. Had distinction of closing the bar at 10:00 on one beer, which was creamy and heavy.

Statue of Liberty in New York harbor

Returned to stateroom and highly pleased to find wires from home: the Foxes, Sally, Bill Dempsey, Charley Jicka, Ida Burke, and letters from Mary Murphy, Margaret Crane and Rose French. While sensation caused was very pleasant, I had a feeling of mild disappointment in being unable to communicate immediately my great appreciation of such profound thoughtfulness. To be accepted is a wonderful thing.

Everything done for me by others and myself to make the trip a success, I settled into my berth and slept soundly until breakfast.

Holland America's T.S.S. Statendam *in the 1930s*

CHAPTER 2

At Sea

Saturday, June 13

At sea: breakfast ample and good. Fruit juices—cereal—fish—eggs and bacon—rolls, marmalade and coffee.

Ten-thirty a.m. daily serving of hot beef bouillon on deck. To me, after the breakfast mentioned, this seemed the most unnecessary kind of refreshment. Lunch and dinner both varied and large. One may have anything on the menu. Some people take all vegetables listed, some both fish and meat, some triple desserts—ice cream, cake or pies and cheese and crackers. Others two or three portions of any one dessert. Tonight a dance in the third class section, to which we have been invited.

Took place on deck. Night foggy and music punctuated by siren blasts. Reacting to the mixture of tourist and third class patrons: class distinctions necessary and justified. Persons of widely different taste and attainments do not seem to be a lastingly contented group. I felt like a gigolo when it was suggested that I dance consecutively with each girl in the party. The dance is over but I did the usual midnight patrol of the decks bathed in fog.

My thoughts turn to helplessness in the event of a collision and I felt quite resigned, everyone having knowledge of many chances of being saved.

Sunday, June 14

Arose with a start, unable to recall having been called by steward. Quickly dressed and hurried to deck, which was deserted. First thought: everyone is attending Mass. Asked Officer time and he replied "10 minutes uff seex." Mass not until 8:00! Enjoyed universal character of the Mass and manner of devotion. Called on Mrs. Carlton Hills per request of Art Grass. During visit with her in first class lounge I couldn't escape noticing the difference in class furnishings and demeanor of people. First class patrons instinctively feel they are right and correct in all attitudes.

Much sport during afternoon of a perfectly beautiful Sunday. Ocean is calm, breeze mild and cool, ship steady and quiet; passing of the sleek "Normandie" within 150 yards.

Evening: much sport at get-together dinner, with caps, balloons and noisemakers. Big laugh watching older men and women lurching and floundering in attempts to keep balloon in motion.

Dance for Tourist Sections better attended than last evening. We have continuous mirth in watching one "Mistah Robbins of Hahvahd," reputedly a leader of social activity aboard, trying to be graceful and dutifully poised while dancing with the usual unrhythmic and clumsy academic style. Much chatting with Bobbie Hayden of Kansas City, relative to all things.

Monday, June 15

Awake with sound of William Beale showering and the sound of waves and quiet providing nice contrast. First day of any degree of roughness—enjoy slight bouncing and lurching of ship. Long conversations in p.m. with William Beale about life, of which he has seen and lived much.

W.B. stated principle of preventing seasickness is to roll *with* the ship. Remembered similar instructions for airplanes—namely, don't try to right the ship with your stomach. Had long conversation with

Ms. Ashley of Kansas City, a very accomplished linguist who knows J.M. Phelps' book and who is in similar work. Swapped tips with her on speaking. She is of the opinion I could have success as speaker, this from a paid critic cheered me much. Saw the principle of social choice beautifully executed in case of one Mr. S. Angell, a swarthy, portly man from New York, Hollywood, etc. The first night aboard he apparently was determined to capture all virgin femininity by the sheer force of his blatant worldliness. After ten minutes with each woman, each increasingly less desirable, he was completely shunned. We saw him today in all his greasy finesse consorting with a hired maid in lowest class section. W.B. and I remained up until 1:30 over beer and chat.

Tuesday, June 16

Up at 7:30 to attend Mass at 8:00. Surprised at slim attendance even Sunday. Myself and two aged ladies are the only daily attendees.

Reaction: When pleasure and religion clash, to hell with religion. Moved by supremely peaceful attitude of the priest. Looks much like Father Coughlin, the activist priest, famous for his weekly radio broadcasts.

[Editor's Note: Charles Edward Coughlin—1891–1979—was a controversial ultra-conservative Canadian-American Roman Catholic priest from Detroit who was a major power in the U.S. far right wing movement in the 1930s and one of the first public figures to make use of radio broadcasts.]

Weather unbelievably pleasant so made several rounds of deck and played much shuffleboard. Introduced Mrs. Hills to my associates who relieved my conversational burden. W.B. suggested we acquaint ourselves with the meaning of the terms Florian, guilder, mark, franc, lire, concierge, Gendarme, carabiniere. W.B. mentioned to me privately Le Femme Moulin Rouge and Hell and Heaven—a very exclusive place where women with barren husbands select, wine and dine their choice of men for baby's father!!! Mental note: Frankie, here is my opportunity to do right by God and Country.

Have not been able to do any reading. W.B. decided to incorporate as a tour feature the travel prayers graciously given me by Mrs. McBride.

Band aboard from Carleton College in Northfield, Minnesota—poor dancers, below average. Result: Washout. (Thank God I'm out of the "ants-in-the-pants stage!")

Much sun bathing aboard this p.m. Mrs. Hills remarked that the tourist section had best location as to sun and fun. Interesting to note break ups of first day emotional alliances. Very foolish—spend rest of time avoiding each other.

Saw movie "Music Goes Round and Round" punk—but welcomed sound of real band rhythm.

Social life aboard an ocean liner

Had long talk in lounge with a Britisher and an expatriated American who has lived in France for 56 years. Reaction: Something strong about nationality. Englishmen are incurably British with ambiguous replies to political questions. The American, although away for 56 years, tremulously insisted upon his citizenship and was fearlessly critical of Europe. Best British line: All men are human and therefore weak.

Beer and peanuts and so to bed.

Wednesday, June 17
Disappointed in missing Mass after having been awakened at 6:50. Determined to make it tomorrow.

Those interested in interpretations or research work in dreams should take an ocean voyage. I've dreamed scores of things each night—and even during morning or afternoon siestas. They are not as deep or as clear as usual, due perhaps to their great number.

I saw a school of porpoises off the port deck this evening. They appear to be about 3 feet long and weigh about 60-70 lbs. Going at great speed (said to be as high as 60 mph), they regularly dive under and jump over the waves. When 3 or 4 swim and jump together they appear much like hurdlers.

Made a trip to the bridge where all the many mechanisms were displayed. Keeping the ship on its course much the same as a plane. A little pilot light atop the bridge is used to signal by Morse code the name of the ship or to inquire the name of a passing ship. The engine room is a maze of huge engines, tanks and pipes. This is an oil burner so the terribly hard work of coal shovelers is obviated.

Even so, one cannot escape the awful contrast between the lolling, sensuous ease of the cabin passengers with the dirty, sweating and poorly fed and housed, underpaid workers below. One sees the whimsical results of fate, birth, etc. in the persons of these classes. We are reputedly born equal, but it seems the equality stops as soon as it starts. For all the arduous unpleasant work ship's workers do for travelers, the collection for the Seamen's fund should equal or exceed that of the actors.

Learned that icebergs appear 1/7th above the surface and 6/7th below. Float as late as May to a point as far south as New Jersey (in a section probably 500 miles east of New York).

Bet on each race tonight, finally collected for last one.

Dance moved from Second Deck to dining room, which is an improvement but no improvement in dancers or the music. Beginning to think many men abhor dancing because of unpleasant memories. Middle class is rightly termed the balance between the high and low. Our lounge always crowded until early morn with persons of all three classes.

Thursday, June 18

Rose at Steward's call and was happy to make Mass.

Have presumably shamed Bobbie Hayden into attending by terming her a heathen at lunch. It seems to me that the supposed unfavorable reaction of others is responsible for our doing many things—well, it certainly won't hurt her.

Another perfect day. Played shuffleboard with Mr. Müehlenbach of New York—a nice person who likes shuffle boarding but who talks incessantly in a friendly enough way, but who happily is utterly oblivious of the titterings of many of his listeners.

Fed up completely with a cheap uncultured punk of foreign extraction who supposedly made thousands on 5-cent malted milks in New York.

Our waiter is much more the gentleman, but is unceremoniously bellowed at by this dollar worshiper. The waiter very sensibly retaliates by delaying service in our favor and gives him items of food less desirable than ours.

This rat, who sprung from foreign soil, is heatedly objecting to the five-dollar head tax he had to pay Uncle Sam.

Lunch seems to fly on the heels of breakfast but everyone is always ready for it, even after finishing bullion and crackers at 11:00 a.m.

Have yet to succumb to bullion but have proved to be a sucker for four o'clock tea.

This evening I played the part of "Papa" Dionne with girls as quints in fancy dress ball.

Our act tied for first place, but the necessary smoking of W.B.'s pipe almost killed me. Later I talked with W.B. and Bobbie until 1:15 about Europe. On a nightcap tour of the deck I bumped as usual into the very young persons sprawled around the stern of the ship reputedly staying up to see the sunrise (which it didn't this a.m.). Youth must have its inning. I did it once or twice but the occasions were never romantic or biological in nature.

Friday, June 19

Up early on cool, sunless day, the wind very strong. Attended Mass and was pleased to have the priest come over to shake hands and express pleasure at knowing me—which he doesn't—nor I him.

After a curtailed breakfast, I donned a top coat and for the first time my cap. Did one turn around the deck and the prized cap blew off into the ocean. Cheered when W.B. told of a sweet young thing who lost a Paris creation in the same manner.

Look forward out of curiosity to arrival at Plymouth, England, Sunday noon. Ship has a chart outside lounge showing daily progress. Won a couple of bets on the number of miles per day the ship makes. Good line—fools come to scoff and remain to pray (or worship).

The amount of British speech affectations aboard is appalling. Sailors aboard are constantly painting or washing—reminds me of my shop days when I also took pride in my surroundings and worked diligently to keep them clean and attractive.

[Editor's Note: The reference here to "my shop days" relates to my father's work teaching shop classes in his early days at Luke O'Toole elementary

school on the South Side of Chicago. In a truly remarkable coincidence, the school was named after my mother's grandfather and dedicated by her father, William R. O'Toole, alderman of the 14th Ward, in 1927. At this point in time, my parents had not yet met.]

Food consistently of high caliber. Had sweet corn for lunch, which ranked with best I ever tasted. Surprising facts: almost all workers, though miserably underpaid, are married and support families; Captain Fillippo, and several passengers aboard who are Dutch, are descendants of Spanish invaders of Holland centuries ago; though we have a ship full of ladies, no heart interest.

Evening rather cold causing most passengers to haunt the lounge—noted again great comfort a room has when it happens to be the best place to be. Intelligence of most transatlantic voyagers indicated by constant and protracted rounds of discussions covering many subjects. At this stage of the journey desire of cabin and tourist class passengers to restrict freedom of third class most marked. Obvious that third class people *generally* are just that.

A place for watching movies while at sea

Attended movie "Abdul the Damned." And I'll be damned if I attend another. The thoroughly obnoxious Mr. Angell punctuates each and all performances with juvenile sound effects. I had a look in on some marital discomfort when a woman was whiningly complaining of her husband's having "escaped." The fact that he had no place to go did not appear to her a mitigating factor. W.B. and I talked until very late with an angelic secretary for a New York lawyer, who was rigidly observant of Catholic doctrines but pathetically childish in acceptance of many incidental phases of history.

Concluded W.B. and I have much the same philosophy of life, broader and more interesting to us than that of the uncompromising believer.

Saturday, June 20

Up at Steward's shaking and off to Mass, which attracted an overflow crowd of three. Priest, Father Sommers of Kentucky, ringer for Father Coughlin, chatted with me and I marveled at the ease he says features the arrangements to see the Pope—Pius XI. *[Editor's Note: The reference here is to Pope Pius XI, with whom my father did indeed have an audience, he describes later. He is the pope who declared Milwaukee's beloved St. Josaphat to be a basilica, a privileged status it retains to this day.]*

Sleep aboard the boat very necessary and easy. In view of my consistently late chats noticed pronounced fatigue after breakfast. Slept till 12:45 with the usual great number of dreams.

Permitted myself to be dragged into the cast of "The Flying Dutchman," a laughable hodgepodge farce. I played the part of Joseph Cummings, an officious dictator of activities aboard ship. If the one-hour rehearsal of this masterpiece is indicative of its presentation the customers will be rolling out of their chairs onto the floor in a combination howl of rage and tremulous hysteria.

Dinner with turkey as the pièce de résistance being over, I retired to don summer formal for first time on trip.

Contrary to expectations, had full house for farce, which went off in the usual amateur style. Felt some glow in being "formally" announced by Professor Roberts. Had distinct pleasure of opening dance with exotic creature, Miss Bribandy who took part of Nellie from Armentier.

Concluded pleasant evening with Messrs. W.B. and Müehlenbach over several Holland beers.

Sunday, June 21

The day dawned with beautiful sunrise, pleasant coolness. Was late for Mass due to forgetfulness of steward.

Learned our "quint acts" 1st place award would be a special cake prepared by the special order of Commander Filippo, whom we had the honor to meet privately in his office. He is a jovial dignified gentleman who comports himself in a style which is a credit to his calling. Surprisingly, I selected fish for lunch on Sunday. I have acquired a taste for two kinds—kingfish and flounder.

Had farewell visit with Mrs. Hills, who is disembarking at Plymouth tonight. Promised to write or see her in Paris. Much excitement at great increase in number of seagulls flying above and around boat; presently out in distance a white spire which was a lighthouse off Scilly Islands in the Celtic Sea, which are operated by England. They are the location of several lighthouses and the base for some 200 soldiers and sailors, ready for any emergency duty.

Now look forward to sighting Plymouth, not because of any boredom, but for a new experience.

I learn the reason why gulls and other birds present so far out have webbed feet—it permits them to float and swim while far from land. They are a graceful bird requiring very little propulsion.

I believe life aboard ship is the closest most of us will ever get to special position. The ever respectful "sir" the waiter intones as he places each course before you; the assistance rendered you when sitting down or rising; the opening of doors, pausing often, and the placement of lemon and sugar are but a few of the many amenities experienced by the passenger.

Attended last movie of voyage, "It's Love Again," an English production that was quite good. Accompanied leading member of party, Miss Louise Abney of Kansas City, a member of the very select Poets of North America of the World. Her playing of Mrs. Frothingbooth in "The Flying Dutchman" was a gem. Talk later with W.B. as we viewed the lights of Plymouth after anchoring in the bay. Retired at 1:00 a.m. experiencing what seemed a new sensation—a motionless ship.

The Isle of Scilly off the west coast of England

CHAPTER 3

On to Holland—
with short stops in English and French ports

Monday, June 22

Awakened early by shouts, cat calls and sporadic singing. Presently realized it was passengers disembarking to Plymouth in a tender. Thought of dressing and going on deck but thought I'd be late so exercised independence by sliding into hall beside stateroom, climbing on ledge and sticking my head out of the porthole. Right at my nose was the tender. Looking down toward the middle was a gangplank, down which were walking the passengers okayed by British customs men. As each individual was recognized by those at the rail, a shout would go up, as the tender filled up there was a great deal of good-natured kidding between passengers of both boats.

As the tender finally drew away in the murky English dawn, and passengers sang "Auld Lang Syne," I returned to sleep content in possession of a new experience. Provoked when the steward in my room said that it was 9:10, causing me to miss Mass again. Explained he had seen me up at 5:00 and thought I'd better sleep. Okay!

Ship minus 140 passengers seems deserted. Here, just as at schools, beaches, on trains, etc., camaraderie develops between ship passengers which, on parting, one misses. Visited with Father Sommers in the third class section, reaction: terrible.

First Class is quiet, dignified, perfectly appointed, but stiffly formal; third class is noisy, poorly furnished, and vulgarly informal. Convinced that middle class is the best. It is democratic, intelligently administered, tastefully furnished. Its cuisine is the same as first class except for slightly less variety. I have just returned from a salt-water bath, which features fruitless attempts to get soap to lather. The huge tub reminds me of the one at the hotel in Jefferson City, Missouri. Feel slightly puffed and wishful of more legal experience when Mr. Bornstein always addresses me as "counselor."

One knows he is traveling with educated people when he hears the discerning comments of their children. One also notices a decided step up of the services rendered as the ship nears each port of disembarkation, which is only worker's psychology.

"Head Tax," the name we have affixed to that foreign asininity, paid his waiter $1.00. Someday he'll be rich and still more obnoxious.

Tomorrow we dock at Rotterdam and it will be our turn with the tips. I shall try to be fair since a large part of the enjoyment of a trip rests in the contentment of those who serve you.

I take great pride in the fact that these workers and companies exist almost entirely by virtue of the magnanimous character of Americans.

One of the really great thrills of my life occurred this evening at 10:30 when we dropped anchor off Boulogne-Sur-Mer, France, and awaited the tender and the French government authorities.

While waiting in the fading light of day (10:30 p.m.), I sensed a thrilling sensation at the blue, romantic odor of the sea and the harbor. It is a peculiarly enchanting one, stout but not unpleasant.

It roused in my mind the deep-seated feelings ever prompting me to make this voyage. While breathing deeply of its mellowness, many indescribable reflections dating back to my impressionistic youth beat ceaselessly upon my brain. Here I was, gazing at a foreign shoreline, on an ocean liner receiving an inner satisfaction for which I had waited almost 20 years. I fervently wished those minutes could be extended infinitely. Presently a pert little tug came tooting alongside and up a rope ladder laboriously crawled a fat French official.

Hauled over the rail by Dutch sailors, he shouted an official but cheery "Bon Jour, Monsieurs." Shortly after, the tender and another larger tug glided alongside. This latter was for the hauling of two cars, the removal of which by pulleys was most modern and interesting. All those leaving the boat had to have their passports and visas okayed by the French officials. When all, including "Head Tax," who was trembling in fearful anticipation of being rejected because he had failed to obtain a French visa (and which worry ruined the trip for him and his fat wife) were accepted, they began to file on board the tender to the farewell shouts of those remaining aboard.

I noted the happy greetings of the French sailors aboard the tender and that our passengers, including the Rev. Father, were throwing cigarettes to them, which they grabbed for eagerly. When finally all was completed, the three boats with short toots, started for shore and our good old boat saluted with the deep, mournful dirge characteristic of ocean liners. I loathed the idea of a change of scene. As the boat started again on its course, I elected to remain on deck breathing in deep draughts of odorous foreign air.

Looking forward, I noticed a brilliant light blue patch of sky. I raced to the bow to absorb more of the impression. There was a gentle wind blowing toward me, which seemed to carry with it the odor of the farms of France, and that also brought me back many years to my pleasant farm vacations in Illinois. A faint suggestion of red in the far western sky caused me to think of the Great War and the fact that the wind I so enjoyed had blown over the graves of millions of dead men buried in France.

It also suggested the imminence of another great Holocaust brought senselessly because of the selfishness of men and the unwarranted greed for power.

[Editor's Note: My father's poignant reference to the graveyards in France likely was prompted by an experience he had as a 12-year-old boy awaiting the return of his brother, Harold, from World War I. When word arrived with the details of Harold's arrival date and his transportation, my father was sent, along with the family dog, a collie named Prince, to hide near the Englewood train station, about a mile away from their home on 58th and Union nearby. Upon seeing Harold emerge from the train, he was instructed to run home and alert the family so they could all hide and be ready to jump out and surprise the war veteran when he opened the door. It was a memorable event that my father loved to talk about for the rest of his life.]

Author, left, pictured with his brother Harold and four of their sisters

As the ship wended its way forward the air became cooler and sweeter smelling, intoxicating me to such an extent that I remained alone at the prow of the boat until I was wet and chilly. Were it not that I was to be locked out there for the night I should still be there. My only regret in this whole wondrous time (1½ hours) is that I could not record the countless impressions as they suggested themselves to me.

I retired, but reluctantly for fear I should miss some new bit of coastline or some sights typically foreign.

Early in the evening while standing on the bridge with Father, I received a bit of a compliment from him to the effect that he admired my English. I do hope to God I can do something worthwhile with it. Such comments imbue me with a feeling akin to power and I only hope that fate will see fit to provide for me a vehicle for its use.

[Editor's Note: Fate, as assisted by a dedicated and disciplined work ethic, was indeed kind to my father, who went on to be the chairman of his high school's English department and a prolific writer and speaker.]

Windmill, Holland

CHAPTER 4

Dutch Treat—
sights and sounds of Holland

Tuesday, June 23

Awakened by W.B. at 7:20 to see "Hook of Holland," the first sight of Dutch land and a large but treacherous harbor leading to the Maas River on which Rotterdam is located. *[Editor's Note: The "Hook of Holland" is a cape and the harbor it forms is on the southwest coast of the Netherlands.]* The farmlands looked beautifully green and well kept. The houses neatly designed, spotless and practical. Very busy port, scores of ships and tugs darting about. Looking over riverbank to roads, saw hundreds of bicyclists of all ages. Holland has a population of 7 million and has 4 million bikes!

After killing time waiting to dock, during which the true Dutch sincere emotion evidenced itself in the frantic wavings and shoutings, accompanied by plentiful tears (during which I saw many ladies who reminded me of my mother and making me wish again we could have been more appreciative and demonstrative as a family), we finally had the thrill of walking down the gangplank for the first time after being cleared by customs, which merely piles cases at sections of a long table and looks or neglects to look inside, and then we were off in a large open car for spots of interest.

Stopped for lunch at Hotel Du Passage at The Hague. It is truly an old world hostelry with large silent beams, high vaulted rooms, heavy furniture and large chandeliers. We were served a delicious steak dinner and had strawberries as large as plums for dessert. We were attended by the Hoffmeister, a portly Dutchman, and a fully liveried waiter. It was a close approach to grandeur.

Arrived at Hotel Carlton at 5:00 p.m. and were breathless at its beauty and the perfection of its service. Marble bathrooms, huge cabinets, lights at all angles, big, deep beds.

Hotel Du Passage, in The Hague

When the "lift" boy admits you and then lets you out of the elevator, he steps completely out until you are in.

Dinner tonight at 7:30 in a room of marvelous wonder. The waiters in immaculate garb, several head waiters in tails, to serve you personally. A superb ensemble to play classics. Perfect service and perfect food. New idea—candied orange skins (very thin) in rich dark meat gravy.

Peculiarity—no coffee with dinners. After dinner Bobbie Hayden and I ventured out for a stroll—attracted a ridiculous degree of attention, I believe because of our dress. The sidewalks were about 2½ feet wide in front of stores and streets very narrow. There are many canals in Amsterdam and 200 bridges. To ease ourselves out of range of stares, we strolled to the Hotel Lido, beautifully located on the bank of a canal, in full view of many interesting buildings, signs, etc. Nice place, well furnished, immaculately garbed waiters,

Bridges and canals in Amsterdam

and six-piece ensemble and band. After having coffee, the ensemble suddenly became a dance band, so we stayed and danced.

Crowds look rather cosmopolitan, but dress dowdy. Much labored dancing and free spending. I tried not to look ridiculous in paying the bill in U.S. money. Don't know now what the bill was or the tip, but gave $2.00 and got back some change. Walked back to the Carlton Hotel and more stares. Reluctant to retire amid such splendor, but see as I look at the decorative electric clock on the wall that it is 1:10 a.m. so, so long.

Wednesday, June 24
Amsterdam—population 750,000—10 percent Jewish people who are mainly in the diamond business. City is the diamond center of the world. Past and present slump has thrown 2,000 diamond cutters out of work. Seventy percent of the vehicles in Holland are of U.S. make, with the tax on them only 10 percent. Practically all hotel attachés attired in formal clothes—and they light your cigarette immediately.

Diamonds take three days to cut through and one week to polish. Wooden shoes cost 50¢, 60¢ and 75¢. Not commonly worn now, except by farmers, highly conducive to the growth of corns.

Grace Moore (a famous operatic soprano from Tennessee) stayed at our Hotel Carlton. Gave concert last night and Hollanders frenzied with enthusiasm.

The hotel has neat plates upon which are painted figures of chefs, maid and bellhop beside a push button. If you want any of these people you merely signify by the button and lo and behold they are at your side.

Rijks Museum—Rembrandt, Jan Steen, P. Rubens, El Greco, Goya, and Dutch painters.

Rembrandt's "The Night Watch"

1st—Rembrandt masterpiece "The Night Watch," an enormous oil painting.

2nd—Frans Hals, merry vivacious face liner. One of the best paintings: "The Merry Drinker" (or "Jolly Toper"). Painted 200 portraits.

3rd—Jan Steen specialized in joyous, humorous situations and happy family life.

Holland's campaign vs. drunken drivers—picture of vehicle and it says Chauffeurs!!! Alcohol?? Nien!!!

Most flats edging on street have "busy bodies"—mirrors fastened to windows enabling persons to watch passers-by without being in the windows. They can sit in an easy chair out of sight and watch the people walking by. All the buildings have arms jutting out near the roof. At the end of this arm is a hook. The whole thing is there for moving furniture in and out of windows. The fact that they interfere with architectural scheme not considered. Windows in stores and particularly taverns may be as long as 12 feet yet will be raised and lowered like ordinary windows.

Wine served with bottle in basket. You merely hold the handle of the basket when pouring. Salt spread by tiny spoon and disk. (Aboard ship, shakers have one large funnel out of which salt streams.)

With ice cream or parfaits the spoon is flat with a straight front edge.

Visited "Volendam," the typical Holland fishing village on the former Zuiderzee, once a shallow but wide bay of the North Sea. All inhabitants in traditional costume, wide, flurrying pantaloons, tight fitting, square-necked blouses and small peaked, jaunty black

Windmills in Holland's countryside

caps with black or natural wood shoes. I learned that the Zuiderzee, which was separated from the North Sea years ago by a series of dams and dikes and made into a fresh-water lake, is to be reclaimed and made into the 12th province (state).

All hotels and public buildings in Holland have orange flags flying from mast (denoting allegiance to Dutch Parliament's ruling Order of the House of Orange, the royal family of the Netherlands).

Within space of 100 feet are: 1) electric and steam railway; 2) streetcar tracks; 3) road; and 4) sidewalk and bike track, giving impression of being hell-bent for somewhere but actually merely a conservation of space. Most ferries in Holland are operated by local governments and are free to all. On the island of Marken on Zee, boys and girls wear long hair until age 6. Later boys have mark on top of their caps to distinguish them from girls.

At 17, girls have hair on the back of the head trimmed but the sides curled. Volendammers wear long pantaloons, and Markensites wear short ones to the knees. Islanders and fishermen and tourist groups will pick up American slang easily.

Went last night with W.B. and Louise Abney to visit Zac, Manager of the Grand Victoria Hotel. He was dressed in typical old world fashion, serving more wine as soon as glasses were empty. Though the morning call was for 6 a.m. we did not retire until 1:30 a.m.

Streetcars in Amsterdam have mailboxes fastened to their rear. The Dutch guilder is the money leader of the world due to Holland's being on the gold standard. Where formerly Americans received two guilders, 50 cents for a dollar, they now receive one guilder, 40 cents for a dollar.

Beers, wines and liquors are surprisingly high—beer, for example, never cheaper than 15 cents per glass. Have noted that in all the European hotels thus far, the maid always enters the room during dinner hour. She fixes the bed for the night and places conveniently pajamas, robe and slippers.

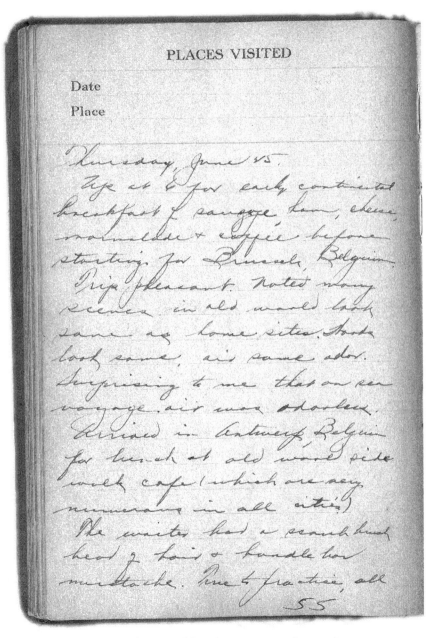

Frank J. Daily's original handwritten journal entry for June 25, 1936

CHAPTER 5

Off to Belgium

Thursday, June 25

Up at six o'clock for early continental breakfast of sausage, ham, cheese, marmalade and coffee before starting for Brussels, Belgium.

Trip pleasant. Noted many scenes in old world look same as sites at home. Woods look same. Same odor. Surprising to me that on sea voyage air was odorless. Arrived in Antwerp, Belgium for lunch at old world sidewalk café (which are very numerous in all cities). The waiter had a scrub brush head of hair and a handlebar mustache.

True to practice, all food is brought to the adjoining table and waiter serves each individually. Old fashioned saloons and dining rooms are still fashionable here.

Arrived and went through Brussels to Waterloo, about 10 miles south. Here I visited the monuments of the 250-foot dirt pyramid built on the spot of the fatal elevation and ditch which ruined Napoleon. The pyramid is made of dirt taken from fatal mound and was erected entirely by women who worked for 15 cents a day hauling dirt for this huge monument.

Returned to Brussels, which is spelled both as Brussels and Bruxelles also, and located at the Atlanta Hotel. Saw all sights of the city, including the Regal Palace. The king is in residence when the National flag of red, yellow and black is flying the mast and soldiers

The Lion of Waterloo in Belgium

were passing to and fro in front. Belgian soldiers wore uniforms much like our own khaki. They are very young and carry themselves poorly. The Belgian people appear to me to be almost a dying nationality. Languages and customs seem to be mixed up among Dutch, German, French and Belgian.

They are not animated and do not seem emotional. The girls however present a striking contrast to those of Holland. They are uniformly chic, pretty and of very attractive physique. Almost without exception they wear cotton stockings.

As usual however the women seem quite up to date in style and the men, for the most part, dowdy. Life in these big European cities seems no different than our own. They have movies of all kinds, concerts, night clubs and taxi dance halls.

Got insights into inexperience and lack of information of our group when they titteringly discovered the public urinals. It is a common sight to see an old man or young boy (even accompanied by his mother) urinating into the street gutter.

Brussels is a huge city of over 1 million. It has mile after mile of 5-6 story buildings all packed one against the other. It seems to have room for many more. Its buildings are very old and look it. They say that it is considered almost a sacrilege to clean the exterior of them. It has many hundreds of buildings built in true modernistic style, which is used to sterling advantage the colored glass windows of many simple but attractive designs.

Belgian currency value is low. One Belgian franc is worth 3.5¢— 100 of their centimes make only one franc. Prices are high however and business in all public lines seems very good.

Belgian political parties are rabid, paralyzing any progress of the government. Communistic meetings are frequently held.

American cigarettes, particularly Lucky Strike and Philip Morris, are made by a British subsidiary and are very hot and strong.

Regret exceedingly the necessity for bath and early bed for another 6:00 a.m. call—the beautiful ladies filling all the streets ought to have a companion.

Berlin during the 1936 Summer Olympic Games

CHAPTER 6

Travels through Nazi Germany —cities and countryside

Tuesday, June 26

Up at 6:00 again for departure for Cologne (Köln). Impressed at the station by the number of Belgian soldiers and officers taking trains and their singular unattractiveness. First experience in compartment trains with aisle free along one side. They are nice for a group to ride in, since they provide privacy. I tried hard to envision war scenes through the territory but didn't succeed very well—18 years is a long time.

At Aix-la-Chapelle, or Aachen, as the Germans called it (and I remember frequent war dispatches from it), the German border was reached. Two burly mustachioed officers came aboard to examine our effects. When one came into our compartment sputtering German, I raised my hands in a gesture of futility. He said, "Ainglis? Ainglis?" I replied, "Nien!" "Americans Americans!" He smiled and readily dropped our bags with an "ok."

The station at Cologne is a huge shed with two glass ends and a glass roof, both of which have powerful designs and beautiful advertisements done in stained glass. Our concierge met us and we trooped over to the Metropole Hotel.

Just outside the station I stopped to gasp at the sight of the famed Cathedral. To date, it is the most inspiring sight of my life. It is so huge that it could easily house 3 or 4 of our own large churches. Some parts of it are 700 years old. It is a peculiar sensation viewing statues made by human hands so very long ago. The size and color of the stained glass windows set records for any church. Most of the rare, treasured ones were removed for the duration of the last war. Many were donated by King Ludwig of Bavaria in 1846, when he was insane. The whole cathedral is pure Gothic and sets the pace for the world.

[Editor's Note: On August 2 and 3, 2016, while in Germany to attend the wedding of an AFS student who lived with us while attending Whitefish Bay High School in 2001-2002, my wife and I traveled to Cologne. There we saw the magnificent Cathedral, which purports to have the tombs and relics of the Magi. We observed the awesome beauty of the stained glass windows, which had been taken out and stored safely in a bunker to protect them from the bombing in WW II, and the statues of the Crucifixion as so accurately described by my father 80 years ago. We also toured the beautiful and imposing railroad station with its classic glass roofs and sides. Today the ads have been replaced by countless stores and shopping areas of all kinds.

[U.S. pilots had orders to avoid bombing the Cathedral, although it was hit 14 times. It has been substantially rebuilt, as has the surrounding area, which was reduced to rubble in the war. When my father saw it 80 years ago, the Cathedral had been under construction for 700 years. Now it has been under renovation and repair for 70 years.]

High up in the myriad crevices and alcoves outside (the capacity is 22,000 people with vast aisles and alcoves) one can see the white tips of full-sized angel wings. Many of the royalty in ancient times paid to be buried there and there are also archbishops interred. The statues of the Crucifixion, done in 1200, show a more haggard Christ, with feet apart and arms drooping, the whole body sagging

The Cathedral amidst the rubble

The Cathedral after Cologne was rebuilt

more than the modern representation. One could spend weeks and weeks in merely gazing at this wondrous sight and never in a lifetime finish describing it.

I had my first foreign hair cut today. The method is similar to ours except surplus hair on top is removed with a comb and razor. Finishing of the side and rear outlines are done without lather.

I viewed Cologne until I could scarcely move. If ever a city deserves rave notices this one does. I do think I could like it more than Chicago. Its shops, hotels, restaurants, advertising, are eminently modern.

Streets are narrow but clean and even shiny. Cars are made small because of the narrowness of the streets. Ford makes standard and reduced-size cars. People walk either on sidewalks or the street. Because of the narrowness of the streets, illumination is down the center. There is a great prevalence of beautiful neon signs on all streets, which gives the appearance of a carnival, most colorful.

The air is sweet and wholesome.

I have observed Nazi storm troopers, policemen, officers of all kinds swarming around. They seem to have nothing to do, but they do look important and are considered so. The "brown shirts" have light brown corduroy pants and black riding boots and look jaunty and Americanish. The officers have a blue ensemble and get a ready salute from all the troopers.

People here are a great improvement over the sluggish phlegmatic Belgians. They seem busy and quite contented. The store displays, particularly in hardware, foodstuffs, bakery goods, candies and ice cream, are the finest anywhere. They are original, modern and highly effective. Food and service all over is the very finest.

People and the general attitude seem unconcerned about war. They neither fear nor think about it. Adolf Hitler's picture appears countless

Nazi troops in formation

Italian dictator Benito Mussolini (Il Duce) with Adolf Hitler in Munich

times in every photography shop, as well as do soldiers in helmets of the last war. Play soldiers for children make them appear the same as in the last war and effectively show them in all possible war activities.

I suppose we like a place because it has those things that we like in it, so I greatly loathe the thought of leaving Cologne with its fresh, fragrant air, breathtaking cathedral, beautiful shops and restaurants, picturesque streets and continental atmosphere.

I've realized my ambition to sleep in a high-vaulted chamber with long, draped windows. The sound of their being drawn back and the influx of the sun's rays are highly intriguing. Also, the extremely long day is an interesting discovery. To have blue sky brilliance from 3:00 a.m. until 10:30 or 11:00 p.m. is rare.

Most hotels have very large rooms with two doors. One inside the other, both very heavy and regal-looking. Few have baths but sinks are at least three times as large as those in the U.S. hotels. Very few provide soap. Butter usually has to be specially ordered and coffee is served for breakfast only.

Our hotel had bathroom innovations in an adjustable round mirror with a circle of light at the bottom to provide close scrutiny of the face during shaving and for makeup for ladies.

Saturday, June 27

We arrived in Koblenz, another famous war-name town at 11:00 a.m. this morning after a comfortable and speedy train trip from Cologne.

I saw thousands of brilliant red swastikas flying from houses, palaces, stores, hotels, streets. We drove up to the hotel Koblenzer Hof which had the appearance of a staff headquarters during war.

We marched through the main doorway, which was guarded by three blue uniformed helmeted Nazis. Inside hundreds more were milling around, gawked at by hundreds of onlookers inside and out.

It is very impressive to see powerful cars drive up and unload smartly dressed officers. The Nazi salute was given at least 500 times during my 20-minute observation. What all these Nazis do is a compelling mystery to me. They are always on the go but never seem to do anything more specific than running around.

While at luncheon I gazed across the Rhine and saw the famed fortress on top of a high hillside called Ehrenbreitstein.

It looks medieval and is specked here and there with red swastikas. Across the Rhine at this point is a type of pony bridge, made up of floating boats, the center of which travel backward and to the side to provide open channel for river traffic.

A statue of Kaiser Wilhelm is located on a point which juts out into the Rhine. It portrays him on a fiery steed, he in a war-like attire and his face matching the mode of the dress. Beside him is a German maiden carrying the crown on a pillow.

These Germans must still feel a reverence for him or for what he represents.

I witnessed tonight a Nazi celebration parading. At about 10:30 p.m., a mammoth fireworks display was given, concluding with a tremendous salvo of explosions and illumination with Roman candles on all the buildings of the fortress Ehrenbreitstein. Then followed, in front of the hotel, a concert by a Nazi band with Nazi soldiers encircling it with flaming torches. As the concert neared its finale the immense crowd of Nazis and civilians began to sing. Loud, clear, deep-voiced Germans sang as though each was the symbol of the state.

For the final selection of "Deutschland Über Alles" a touching hush fell over the multitude. As the music rose in pitch, a sea of arms flashed forward and the voices and music beat upon the eardrums in terrific volume. After the concerts a huge mob betook itself to various drinking places to spend the remainder of the night in dignified celebrating. Nazi officers were very friendly and took every opportunity to explain again and again the principles of their movement and the love they feel for "Der Fuehrer."

I cannot escape the feeling that this huge mob of men belonging to a party based definitely on socialistic principles involving individual sacrifice and contributions to the state, is but a potent nucleus for war. They dress, act, feel, live, think and talk like soldiers.

Sunday, June 28
Up at 7:30 at hammer on the door by the concierge. Peculiarly this splendid avenue hotel is without telephones in the rooms. I went to Mass at a church in the shadow of the Kaiser's statue. I was surprised, in view of Nazi campaign against religion, to find many Nazis in attendance.

The head usher, who might possibly be a priest, was dressed in a flaming red robe trimmed with black stripes down the center and around the neck, wearing a hat something like a bell hop's, but flaring wide near the top and carried a black staff surmounted by a gold knob.

Back to the hotel already crowded with Nazis and prepared to go aboard a Rhine steamer Kaiserin Frederica for a trip to Wiesbaden. Nazi officers, smitten with a couple of our girls, visited until the last minute repeatedly mentioning that "American-German" girls should settle in Germany and help "re-stock" the fatherland.

We had a pleasant and highly picturesque trip down the Rhine with mountainsides ingeniously cultivated for grapes on either side. In the misty vastness here and there an ancient fortress or castle, down near the shore there were modern hotels and swimming places.

We went to the magnificent Kaiserhof Hotel in Wiesbaden with a famous German spa. It is in a secluded section, away from the city hustle, a quiet, dignified, but perfectly gorgeous palace actually used by the Kaisers. At dinner we were placed at a long table, the center of which was terraced with beautiful and fragrant roses. We were waited upon by three suave gentlemen in tails.

My commonplace station in life would not permit me to forego tipping 50 pfennigs, although the tip is already included in the bill.

Marksburg Castle, high above the Rhine River

The luxury Kaiserhof Hotel

Later, W.B. and I had coffee at a sidewalk café on the boulevard. Back to the Kaiserhof. I purchased a bottle of choice Marseille wine. W.B. and I shared it with three of the girls on a quiet balcony outside their room. After returning to the room, I could feel the hushed grandeur of the place, its immense halls and grand staircases with a regal splendor designed for royalty and rich, the intrigue which must have featured its wartime existence. At breakfast there were more roses surrounded by three American flags.

Last night W.B. and I became boulevardiers and sat in a café sipping coffee. I noted that here, when a couple walks, the woman is always on the outside. We return to our sacred precincts and sniffed much cool, fragrant air.

Monday, June 29

Reluctant to rise from richly appointed bed in such exalted surroundings.

The mob went to the Henkell champagne plant in the a.m. "Takes at least four years to prepare for consumption."

It is kept in vaults (open) 90 feet below ground level with bottles lying on their side, bottom end slightly elevated. As it matures it is shaken to mix thoroughly. At first fermentation yeast is added. After further maturing it is again shaken and other wine and yeast are added. Grapes here are grown on a slate base while those in France have a chalk base, making French products sweeter but inferior.

This p.m. we took the bus to Frankfurt un Main to see the von Hindenburg. It was amusing to hear the driver call out points of interest in deep German and to look and to wonder what there was about the thing to cause such gesticulation.

Arrived at airport, which is well watched and guarded. Private roads lead in for the last 1½ miles. As we approach we see signs posted at numerous places with the words "rauchen verboten!"

(smoking forbidden). This is because of the inflammable hydrogen used in the Zeppelin. To step inside the door of the hanger and have this incalculably huge monster reaching from the top of a sky-high hanger right down to you is disconcerting. The flaming red Nazi emblem on the tail flares in vivid contrast to the gray of the bag. The place is humming with activity in preparation for 8:00 p.m. take off for the U.S. (It is now 4:00 p.m.)

Cost to view the Zeppelin was 5 pfennigs; cost for dish of ice cream was 50 pfennigs. The experience of viewing the large ship in the hanger is different. One gets the idea of its colossal proportions. I mailed a letter and two cards for transport by the Hindenburg. A letter cost one mark, 35 pfennigs, the cards were 75 pfennigs.

[Editor's Note: On May 6, 1937, less than a year after my father had viewed the Hindenburg, the hydrogen-filled airship—the largest aircraft in the world at the time—caught fire in a landing attempt at Lakehurst Naval Air Station in New Jersey, falling to the ground in a ball of flames, incinerating in 34 seconds. Of the 97 people aboard, 35 perished. A newsreel of the horrific crash was broadcast in theaters around the world.]

The Hindenburg over New York City

The crash of the Hindenburg in New Jersey

Went through Mainz and Frankfurt on the way back. Both reminded me of Amsterdam. Music and flowers everywhere. The universal use of window boxes and blinds on windows create a stylish continental atmosphere. One finds flower gardens, cafés, playgrounds even along the riverbanks. One long triangular-shaped place at Frankfurt had a large area for refreshments, one for tennis, roller skating, swimming. The whole of it festooned with seasonal flowers. They merely capitalize on the necessity for space utilization.

Had champagne dinner tonight, the donation of W.B. and myself. Atmosphere too amateurish for meaningful appreciation. W.B. and I again ducked out for a frolic of our own. Got to the hotel late and had to pack for early departure. Becoming more expert at packing. Experience always tells.

Tuesday, June 30

Reluctantly left the elegant Kaiserhof Hotel with great expectations of Heidelberg.

Driven to the station by Karl König, Kaiserhof Chief Foreign Relations Officer. The car, typically low slung, had poor riding and loud sounding motor. Noticed many of European makes have rear wheels on a low-legged angle. The Opel seems to be the German Ford.

Some miscellaneous observations: I have noted an astounding degree of baldness in Germany. Some haircuts are like those of my Negro friends (all bald in the back with a hedge fence sticking up in front); summer clothes on natives are extremely rare. Straw hats never seen; prevalence of glasses wearing by men.

The train to Heidelberg was a good one, comfortable and fast with very few stops. The station is another large, airy one with stained glass effects.

Went on to Europa Hotel to wile away some time until lunch. Went across the street to the Victoria Hotel for Heidelberg beer, very good, light but of distinctive flavor. Veranda is beautifully modern, light and airy. Functionaries with white tie and tails are ever hovering near. After lunch I took a trip by bus around Heidelberg. Beautiful city situated on high sides on either side of the Neckar River.

Heidelberg was founded in 1386 and it was originally built and operated by Jesuits. The Jesuit church is still nestled among the original buildings. The Jesuits were driven out during the Reformation and it is now operated under Protestant auspices. We visited buildings on the grounds (the rest are scattered around the city) and also a student jail. It is considered an honor to be jugged for some offense. The staircase and room proper were studded with silhouettes, signatures, sayings, dates. Some scratched on, others painted or burnt on by candle fire.

Many of Germany's great names appear there, among them Count Johann von Bernstorff, an Ambassador to Washington, D.C., at the time of our entrance into the world war.

The Red Ox Inn is merely a beer parlor flush with the street, having beer tables, chairs, German scenes and faces pictured on the walls. Proprietors are descendants of many generations in the same place. It is a shrine for all old grads who invariably head there on arrival.

The garden, the scene of love of the Student Prince and waitress, is outdoors facing the road, which is covered with overhanging vines. Heidelberg Palace, the largest fortress in Europe, which was built by the ruling princess of Palatine (a province) is on the side of a mountain and commands a view of the river and countryside. Partly in ruins since 1593, partly restored.

I had the same intriguing thrill I always experienced in boyhood book days when climbing winding stairways, winding our way through tunnels, peeking out gun holes, etc. Kitchen is typically huge, with 50-foot high, extremely wide chimney place. Wine cellar is festooned with Christmas tree branches that gave off that wonderful Christmas pine odor.

One huge barrel, around which I climbed on a high stairway, has a capacity of 50,000 gallons. Part of one section (the typical round turret corner) was blown up by the French and still rests on the hillside where it fell. Its name covered with vine growths. Many bridges, towers and buildings built in medieval times, still are used. The town reeks with tradition. We left at 5:30 p.m. aboard a fine train for Nüremberg. The train was new and modernly furnished. A fine feature of it is that you can stand before the open windows in a passageway outside of the compartments. Arrived tired but expectant in Nüremberg, the toy center of the world, at 10:30 p.m. Went to the Nüremberg Wüerttemberger Hof Hotel. A room on the top floor with window ledges which were bedecked with flowers.

The room faced on a court, which gave a view of three sides of the building and the vine-covered beer garden below—very atmospheric.

Wednesday, July 1
Awakened by the demands of nature after a restful sleep. Started to sense the usual lack of room-toilet facilities in practically all of European hotels, along with their continued failure to provide soap. Breakfasted at 9:45 and noted the usual large number of young men and boys moving about doing a variety of dining room chores. The attitude of superiors toward them is uncompromisingly exacting. Their lot is one of long years of faithful, efficient service with little recognition.

Our party was free until one o'clock lunch. Strolled about the streets, breathing in old world atmosphere. Statues and fountains show unusually faithful treatment and execution of body shapes. Usual large number of "Konditorei," which are places for light refreshments. Pastries, ice cream, coffee, candy. All are neat, clean and very attractive. Due no doubt to the passive nature of these people near Bavaria, the Nazi salute is given everywhere with great frequency, even by civilians.

I noted a decided change in the style of dress. Alpine, feathered hats are very common. One costume is very common: Goat skin shorts, five-inch pieces of knitted stocking, which fit like a band around calf of the leg, a button jacket of light material and an alpine hat.

The German custom is to wear a gold band wedding ring on the right hand. Engagement rings are worn on the left. German money is easy to become accustomed to—the mark and pfennig are the same as a dollar and cent. One hundred pfennigs equals one mark.

Cigarettes are shorter here, flat, have sweet, fragrant odor, are mild, burn faster, white ash, and cost at least one mark (40 cents) per package of 25.

I toured the quaint streets of Nüremberg this afternoon. The streets are cobblestone, houses are stone with red tile shingled roofs.

Tile appears to be blackish-orange in color and very picturesque. The town still has ancient tower entrances, original walls, moats. A castle, perched on the hillside, has a view of all the surrounding country. At distant points one can see towers, which were used to signal messages. Torture chambers contain all appliances used: eye gougers, spiked chairs, body stretchers, skin tearers, bone breakers and body choppers. Due to constant repair, some of the zest for things typically ancient was lost.

Churches are very large, detailed and symbolically ornamented. Facades are particularly heavily statued.

Faces appear too large and are frequently smiling. Christ in many pieces appears stout. Adam and Eve usually found on either side of entrance are nude, save for a fig leaf, at times appearing happy, other times ashamed.

Toy stores are really toy stores, containing nothing but toys, dolls, etc. All are in fine proportions, well built and attractively painted and dressed. Railroad stations here provide for different classes. First and third class restaurants in some stations serve different food, charge different prices. Nüremberg, with its very quiet atmosphere, narrow streets in many parts outlined by churches and buildings has a definite European atmosphere.

[Editor's Note: Nüremberg would gain great significance in the rise of Germany's Nazi Party. Massive national conventions—known as the Nüremberg Rallies—were held annually in the streets as Adolf Hitler rose to power. At the 1935 rally, Hitler as Chancellor and Fuhrer, pressured the German Reich's legislature to pass the anti-Semitic Nüremberg Laws, which revoked German citizenship for Jews and other non-Aryans. In the buildup to World War II, the city became the center of the German Reich and a site for weapon production, including aircraft, submarines

Nazi soldiers in formation at a national rally

and tank engines. Following the war—and a heavy bombing campaign of the city by the Allies—German officials who were accused of war crimes and crimes against humanity stood before an international tribunal in the Nüremberg Trials.]

Thursday, July 2

It is surprising how alike are all days on a trip. Saturday and Sunday create absolutely no difference in feeling. Every night seems to stretch forth infinitely—a whole city and its people to see and learn—anticipation of each new adventure very zestful.

Travel Truths: at a certain point one becomes satiated and ceases to record impressions; a traveler needs lots of rest because rapidity and number of impressions is a tax on the nervous system.

[Editor's Note: This observation explains why my father did not include every city or locale he visited in his journal. For example, he

frequently recalled over the years his observations, impressions and expe-
riences during his visit to Berlin, which was hosting the 1936 Olympics
at which Jesse Owens, the famous African-American sprinter from Ohio
State, vanquished his German opponents to the great dismay of Adolf
Hitler and his supporters.

[In particular, my father described an encounter he had at the Olympic
Stadium with a group of Nazi officers who wanted him to stand and give
the Nazi salute—"Heil Hitler." My father refused, telling them that the only

Jesse Owens won the gold medal four times in the 1936 Olympics

flag he would stand to salute was that of the United States. If he had taken
that position a few years later I would not be here to tell this story!]

Arrived in Munich (spelled here "München") at the Regina Palace Hotel in time for luncheon in another high-windowed, heavily carpeted formal dining room.

The maître d'hôtels here (Europa) are nervous, high-strung persons, who groan when one of their myriad of frustrated underlings makes the slightest noise. Due to large influx of English and Americans, most all of them speak English and have a high degree of pride in announcing items on the menu. This afternoon we went sightseeing about the city viewing modern airport, palaces, old world city entrances, statues, galleries, museums. W.B. and I went to a hoffbrau where it is fashionable to bring along a sliced white radish to eat while drinking beer from a stein at least two-and-a-half times as large as ours. The place is frequented by Bavarians dressed in native costumes who sing out their songs in loud voices.

The place is huge, seating at least one thousand and is said to have been the scene of Hitler's unsuccessful Putsch of 1923. People buy beer, cheese, radishes, etc. from outside and then prepare a meal after ordering beer.

Later this evening we went to a popular garden to listen to an orchestra play something that sounded vaguely like jazz. We sat drinking port, and suggested to the waiter that the band play "Stardust." This immediately caused this band to ask me questions and to whistle the tune for them. They compromised by playing "Tea for Two" looking straight at me and nodding frequently while playing. When I bought a round of drinks for them I heard many more American tunes.

This morning, I went on a tour of the Art Institute and the Deutsches Museum, the latter the greatest scientific museum in the world. It is said that this museum caused Julius Rosenwald to begin a similar one in Chicago. I was surprised to learn that it contains the original Wright Brothers' machine. All conceivable forms of scientific machine developments were available to view, but such an effort would require a 15-mile walk.

Went to a café across from City Hall to view the wonderful moving, life-sized figures, which moved to music. There are four features: 1) two figures with hammers in hands who hit chimes at 9:00 a.m. and 1:00 p.m.; 2) heralds and banner carriers who are announcing a joust between Bavarian and Polish knights, who are gilded figures in gold armor astride steeds—the second time around the Bavarian topples the pole; 3) on a stage directly below, a group of native Bavarian men dancing, led by a figure in the middle, who acts as a maestro, dance peacefully, representing joy at the end of a plague; and 4) rooster atop both stages flaps wings and crows three times. The whole performance requires 12 minutes.

I've become tired of seeing covered, camouflaged military trucks, a score of different types of uniforms and the Nazi emblem forever flying before my eyes.

Life-size figures of the Glockenspiel in Munich

Took a cab out to the venerable "Englischer Teegarten" by an outdoor spot part of King Ludwig of Bavaria's estate. Six thousand people can be accommodated by 120 waitresses, who draw 22 marks and a few meals per month.

The manager is a former officer in the German army. He recalls the last visit of the Kaiser in flight to Holland. He said men were unmoved by his presence, primarily because, by fleeing, he was proving himself a coward. The Kaiser took 90 million marks with him. Sidelight: Our very expert waiter, who speaks English clearly, gets 110 marks per month. 70 must be paid to the Reich (Hitler), 16 for unemployment relief, 8 for medical fund. His salary is 26 marks.

I have seen the Nazi salute so often that it is difficult to refrain from following suit. A traveler soon finds, however, that despite Hitler's 95 percent vote of confidence, the people are groaning under a terrific tax load.

We arrived at noon at Oberammergau, probably the most famous village in the world. We knew we were there when the cross atop the highest hill was sighted. This cross, which has been there for 300 years, is symbolic of the fame of the village. We were met at the train by charming, civil, kindly Anton Lang, the world renowned "Christus," the Christ figure of the Passion Play, at whose house we were to be guests.

The quiet sincerity of the village and its people (1,600) was deeply impressive as we walked to Lang's home. He is a pottery maker, a hard worker, just as was our Savior, who worked with his hands as a carpenter. One feels exalted in his presence, though he is ever the smiling, warm natural host. Frau Lang is a typical smiling German wife possessing dignity and a sense of proportion. Though he signs his name many times to books, pictures and cards each time he signs for you seems to be your entry into the society of the famous. The play has really been his life and his faith and his love of God is truly touching. He states simply and without fear that he believes he suffered as much on the cross as did Jesus.

In the afternoon I visited the only church, Saints Peter and Paul, and arranged to have some Masses said for my mother. It is a most wonderful church, having no stained glass windows, possibly because the interior is mostly in white and the reflection is heightened by the sunlight. Many of the myriad of statues are chalk white, while others are of the deepest, richest, smoothest gold I have ever seen.

The churches here feature a canopy or ceiling structure, the altar seeming to be set up and back as on a stage. The confessionals are open, only the priest being closeted. When the collection is taken up a little bell tinkles at the bottom of the basket, probably to announce to very seriously devout Germans the taking up of the collection. Masses here cost 2 marks (80 cents).

I attended a fest of some kind tonight (Fourth of July) at the Weingarten, in which typical Bavarian dancing was portrayed. The custom is for the man to select any lady and she dances as he pleases—mostly hopping up and around. At the end of each dance he shakes hands with her (this experience once again affirmed my utter unconcern for yodeling).

I returned home in beautiful moonlight and remained in the open window of my room drinking in fresh sweet air from the moon-drenched hillsides. Marveled again at the complete naturalness of one of God's truly great gentleman sleeping downstairs.

Sunday, July 5

I ate breakfast at 8:20 and then off to Mass at 8:30. The church was packed and I made my way to a pew that seemed to have room. I found myself seated beside my host, Anton Lang, the Christus, a rare thrill. Seats slant in from the back, probably to keep people from drowsing, but I remained erect and motionless out of respect to the deep devotion from Anton Lang. The sermon was 45 minutes long in German. Music, with augmented orchestration, was beautiful and stirring.

Herr Lang escorted our party to the "Passions Theatre," an undecorated, shell-like structure, with open stage over which in the distance the hills form an atmospheric background.

It seats 6,000 people and the seats, which are arranged in three sections, are simple, unappointed pieces of wood. Went backstage, lifted the cross carried by the Christus and visited dressing rooms where, even though the next play was not until 1940, the gowns hang as though it were tomorrow. I made an interesting discovery in the attic of one of the old houses—garments worn by actors in the original play in 1634. All of the materials for the garments come from Egypt and Jerusalem and are their very best. All costumes, scenery and props are designed and made in Oberammergau.

Even music, which is said to equal the best, was composed here. Characters are chosen on the basis of ability, lineage and character by schoolmates and the burgomaster. You can have 600 on stage at one time.

Lang was on the cross for 20 minutes. A famous opera star waited 45 minutes to shake hands with Lang, whom she termed the greatest actor on the world stage. When I presented two cigars to this famous personage his reaction was the same as though a great honor was being bestowed upon him. I met his son, Tony, a professor of German literature at Georgetown University. Characters are not permitted to capitalize in any way on the play and its glory must remain here in accordance with the name it was given in 1634. Oberammergau is beautifully situated in the midst of the most beautiful hills I have ever seen. They have a soft carpet of green covering of their surface, which is studded with Christmas trees, poplars, and tamaracks, so even that they seemed to have been placed as in a design.

Spent a long period again tonight in the open window, intoxicated with the effect of moonlight on the houses and hills. The whole effect seems the essence of peacefulness. In church, one feels he has been there for a number of centuries. In the pleasant quietness, one may hear the tinkle of a cowbell or the mooing of a cow. Suddenly modernity returns with sounds from a bus roaring up with more visitors.

Monday, July 6
Up at a knock on the door, a call from these people one simply cannot ignore.

Then to a cheerful breakfast to be greeted by the sweet gentility of Anton Lang, ever solicitous for our welfare.

Bading us goodbye he asked us to remember him to our friends visiting in the future. Again, the essence of humility. The anomaly of a really great personage asking that we recommend him to our friends, as to this world, virtue alone is its own reward,

Away to Gaamisch-Partenkirchen and Menden in Germany, and finally Innsbruck, Austria. Mountain scenery is strikingly beautiful all of the way. Still the smooth green carpet of grass from peak to foot, with peaks now be speckled with snow. Crosses are frequently seen on accessible peaks.

Innsbruck is a place of many hotels with fine mountain scenery. Reputedly it is a playground for the elite, but night spots are conspicuously rare. I heard some genuine Tyroleans in real presentation tonight—again I can do without any yodeling.

Austria, like Belgium, seems to lack the vitality of Germany, due again, seemingly, to the mixture or segmentation of the people. Even in Innsbruck the Italian influence in dress, habits and people was apparent.

I visited much with Jack Kemmler, owner of the Tyrol and Europa hotels. Took a full draught of Austrian atmosphere in tall, open balcony doors.

CHAPTER 7

The Italian Alps and Il Duce

Tuesday, July 7

I took the early train for Brenner Pass, Bolzano, and Conettza, Italy, although I nearly missed it due to somnolent propensity of an older couple. As in all other cases, this was an electrified train, starting without warning and running smoothly even over high, mountain passes.

At Brenner's Pass, the Italian border, numerous Fascist officers boarded the train for inspection.

Surprisingly, they took only my bag, which as usual, was valueless. Noticeable that they were not easily satisfied with garbled explanations and talked, shouted and gestured until they were satisfied. They were not nearly so warmly hospitable as were the Germans, although the fact that they were much younger men may account for that.

The uniforms noted were slate, leaning toward green and featured Tyrolean-felt hats with short black brim and long, side turned front brim (one side up, one side down, after the fashion of Al Capone) having a long feather on one side of the crown.

The territory taken from Austria by Italy required 2½ hours to travel through by electric train.

Arrived in Bolzano (formerly Austrian Bozen), and had lunch under a sidewalk canopy, accompanied by scores of pigeons, which strutted under tables and chairs begging food. I noticed that the food was much heavier and of course much less delicate. This is the first place I visited where afternoon siesta closed businesses between 12:00 and 3:00. Siesta is not actually a sleep—merely a rest or a lull, due to pacifying effect of the heat.

We started on our trip to Venice by private bus. Went by pencil thin mountain roads and deep tamarack forests, our eyes feasting on the beauty, symmetry and color of the cliffs, streams and trees.

We arrived mid-afternoon at a beautifully appointed hostelry, the Grand Hotel Carezza al Lago, situated between two devastatingly beautiful mountain peaks.

We had been gazing at these peaks for miles, and to find them providing front and rear views for our hotel was most exciting. The one in front called Latemar is most interesting, being grayish in color, streaked with a sort of bronze color. In gazing at it, as I have for hours, a cathedral, a skyscraper fortress and apartment house are clearly defined. The shapes and splashes of color are so regular as to cause one to term the Latemar's outline as architectural. My first reaction descriptively was "cathedralesque."

The hotel is said to be 25 years old, yet when you step inside you feel as though the whole place was finished but a few hours before. Everything appears new, clean, glossy. The view from every room is breathtaking. Landscaped garden in front, on which a window looks out on a fairyland of Christmas trees beautifully arranged according to size and shape. Separating them are rows of bushes made from the trees but kept trimmed. To compare this place with Jasper Park in Alberta, Canada, is to credit one with a fiendish sense of humor.

Wednesday, July 8

Breakfasted in the room with W.B. but gazing out the window at the beautiful morning view of Mount Latemar. I walked about spacious grounds and marveled at the completeness of services at this gem in the clouds. It is so far away from everything that a stay here as a guest is like a society weekend.

Left after lunch and began the interesting part of our Dolomite trip. Long, winding narrow highways are of fine construction and being improved. We drove past several Austrian Soldiers' Graveyards. They are marked by a black cross and are maintained by Italy. All passes have good hotels and restaurants. Pass Pondar is most interesting in color, shape and height. Dolomites, really part of the Alps, are picturesque because of size, characteristic shapes and variety of coloring. These, coupled with a carpet of green grass and millions of absolutely straight Christmas trees with lacy fringes and trails of fine white snow, make them a sight to be remembered.

We arrived for dinner at the hotel in Miramonti at the pass Cortina d'Ampezzo. It is considered a deluxe hotel and is headed by Mr. Romeo Menaggio, an affable Northern Italian, who is married to an English girl of great beauty. He speaks six languages. He is a fine, sociable host who danced with the girls and treated to a round of drinks. He was greatly upset when I bought a round. He said that I should wait for his arrival in the United States before treating. We talked long about Germany, Dolomites, hotels, cigarettes.

Some trifles: Italian police are dressed in dark blue suits having tail coats, red leg strips, white wrist bands, silver buttons and square Napoleonic hats. These are state police.

Some bathtubs in the hotel have drains extending all the way up to the faucet; some have faucets on the side at the middle of the tub; hotels really do not provide soap and do not provide butter at either lunch or dinner; they do not serve coffee except at breakfast and then only with milk.

As we penetrate deeper into Italy, signs and pictures of Il Duce became more numerous. Saluting is rare, happily so, after the inane frequency of it in Germany. Italy is the most atmospheric and the most European of all countries. Streets, court ways, stores have a romantic atmosphere about them, which is exhilarating. The dress of people is very modern—were it not for the scenery and streets, one could not tell the difference in people.

Thursday, July 9, and Friday, July 10
I got up early and breakfasted in the garden—a new experience, but quite ordinary reaction.

After another sincere and hearty farewell by a squad of hotel attachés, we start our trip to Venice.

We covered, over splendid new roads built by Il Duce in the last few years, 175 km. in 3½ hours. Italy has roads called Autostratas. They are roads without crossings running great distances. They seem to decline gradually toward the south and then to drop off to levelness very suddenly. Italian busses and stations are very much like our own.

Innovation: coffee espresso, (made one cup at a time).

CHAPTER 8

The Splendor of Venice

We arrived at noon at the Adriatic Sea and on to Venice and its canals. The Renaissance is reported to have had its beginning in Venice.

With four others of our party I climbed into a frail, black gondola and was rowed up the Grand Canal to the Hotel Europa. Gondolas travel on the wrong side like French autos. The gondolier yells as he approaches blind corners. We docked at a floating ramp in front of the hotel and were ceremoniously helped out.

A gondola in a narrow Venice canal

After lunch, we spent much time in San Marco Square—an immense outdoor space with historic buildings on all four sides. Among them, the Campanile, a tall finger-like tower of no particular beauty, the Church of San Marco, richly and heavily decorated outside, and the Doge's Palace, a very historic place. I believe that the square could seat 30,000 people. I spent part of the afternoon walking along the Grand Canal. At every block there is a bridge instead of a street crossing. Felt heavy and stuporish all afternoon because of the heat, but at any shady spot there is cool and a breeze.

Beds here have mosquito netting ascending from the bed to the ceiling like a royal canopy, although one of them got inside with me during the night! This netting is said to be necessary.

Italian money:

The base is the lira (9 cents) 100 centesimi.

Lira pieces in 100L, 50L, 10L, 5L, 2L and 1L. Centesimi are in 50, 20, 10. There is difficulty in distinguishing them, however, because there is no connection between the size and value—i.e. a 5L piece and a 20L piece are practically the same size. There is a difference in material, though, that a visitor cannot easily detect.

I visited the Doge's Palace this afternoon, the Ancient Seat of the Venetian Republic. It contains many art treasures and unusually large rooms. Built in 1600, it had a glorious existence, while in ancient times, Venice, as Queen of the Adriatic, ruled the world. The palace is connected to the Bridge of Sighs, which got its name from reports that prisoners sighed as they were led to interrogation rooms and their cells in the adjoining prison.

The palace and churches generally have life-size statues, outlining the front roof. San Marco (the Church of St. Mark) has the famous four bronze horses, which are over 1,000 years old and have been in Turkey, Greece, Venice and France. Their presence has witnessed the downfall of every dynasty—Greek, Venetian, Napoleon and Austria.

Saint Mark's is a vast edifice facing San Marco Square. It has paintings on its outside walls and many statues. In Venice they chose the same orange and black tile roofs seen throughout Europe. Looked at from a height it seems almost like a carpet print. Buildings are built very close together with apparently no idea of regularity. It is a typical old world experience to walk through the narrow court ways, which though only 5 or 6 feet wide are both street and sidewalk.

Saturday, July 11
The day is entirely free. I rise early and breakfast alone. I had retired late due to my again perching at my window gazing at Venice, illuminated by moonlight, a string of lights along the bay and the reflection on the Campanile from San Marco Square.

Campanile bell tower and Doge's Palace, Venice

The bells of churches here strike frequently but softly. I have noted that there seem to be more priests than worshipers and that the people have reverence for neither the faith nor the priests that we have. Most churches have curtains covering the entrances where the doors are open and they have decorative tiled floors, which are uneven and seat small numbers considering their large size.

Took a boat trip to Lido (or "the beach"), considered *the* Lido of the world. It is an island having a long stretch of beautiful beach, thousands of small beach shelters, and several large, luxurious hotels. The Adriatic looked like a picture book with sail boats dotting its sun-brilliant blue waters.

On my return I went on another boat trip down various canals to the other side of the city.

These boats provide remarkably efficient service for 1L (6 cents).

I do feel I've gotten what I should from Venice. I've walked ceaselessly, looked in countless stores, observed everything and breathed the very spirit of the place. The view of the Grand Canal from the water's edge dining floor of the hotel is perhaps the best. When the colored lamps are lighted on each table the effect is enchanting.

I have begun to feel also that Europe is a place for Europeans and that America is the place where we can be happiest. The people here in Italy are being crushed under unbelievably heavy and numerous taxes.

To date, the hotels where I have stayed are:

City	Hotel Name
Amsterdam	Carlton
Brussels	Atlanta
Cologne	Monopol—Metrapole
Koblenz	Kablenger-Hof
Wiesbaden	Kaiserhof Hotel

Heidelberg	Europa
Nüerenberg	Württemberger Hof
Munich	Regina Palast
Oberammergau	Anton Lang's House
Innsbruck	Hotel Tyrol
Carezza	Grand Carezza Al Lago
Venice	De L'Europe

One sees Il Duce's picture frequently, but the attitude among Fascists is much milder than among Nazis. Germany and Italy are working together on trade agreements since Germany did not observe a boycott with Italy. Picture shows still feature heavy indoctrination through scenes of Fascist activity. Managers and concierges at the hotels are more like hosts than officials. The hotels are more home-like and their large staffs are always looking for an opportunity to serve you. The attitude of waiters is much easier here due to the fact that 10 percent is always added to the bill.

I contributed this evening to a worthy cause—our paying a gondolier. After rowing us for about 20 or 30 minutes, I told him "be seated and rest," to which he said "grazie" (thank you). We floated in the steam ship lane of the Adriatic for a while and then told him to return to the hotel. On arriving he haltingly declared the price to be 25 lira ($2.25). I knew it was exorbitant and so did he, but the work is so arduous in nature I was happy to ease his lot. I noticed the joviality of him and two companions a bit later as they ordered wine in one of the narrow court shops. I knew it was at my expense, but was happy for it.

Gondolaing at night is one of the visitor's Venetian "musts" and the thrill is worth any price. Americans are under the impression that everything is cheap in Europe. Nothing could be more erroneous. Our type cigarettes cost at least 35 cents a package and the cigarette is inferior to ours.

P.M. (Friday afternoon) the price of a bit of ice and a small pot of coffee was 48 cents. The price for laundering a shirt ranges from 25 cents to 45 cents.

CHAPTER 9

The Art and Architecture of Florence

Sunday, July 12

Up at 5:00 for early departure for Florence, spelled here "Firenze." The trip to the station via gondola was a fine closing to our stay in Venice. I marveled again at the dexterity of the gondoliers in handling 25 to 30 foot sculls in narrow channels. They turn corners with only about an inch to spare and never touch a building. I leave Venice with a memory of its San Marco Church and Square, the Campanile, the Doge's Palace, the Lido, the aged buildings, gorgeous colorings and individual atmosphere. The styles of architecture here are: Byzantine, Baroque, Gothic and Renaissance.

The train to Florence is one of many throughout Italy that are electrified. Also, they are speeding service remarkably by digging tunnels into the hills. The station at Florence is modern to the minute. Even its printing is modernistic. The date is given as the 13th year (of Fascism) instead of an A.D. date.

Florence is much like a typical big U.S. city. The streets are wide and well paved and lighted. Buildings are large, well designed and constructed. I went to Mass at Santa Lucia Church and have never witnessed such slipshod worshiping.

Florence and its domed Renaissance cathedral

The people here seem to know nothing at all of the mechanics or formal procedures of worshiping. I came to the conclusion that clergy is too thick headed or the people are unable to grasp the idea. Also, the collection was an insult to the maintenance of an institution—conclusion: America is the fatted calf of Catholicity.

I made two discoveries: toilet paper, with one smooth and one coarse side, is in a container with the top covered and is used as an ashtray and cigarette holder. Many places in Florence feature American-type products and services. American products are most common in Europe—e.g. Dr. Scholl's and Palmolive. Outdoor cafés are very common here and feature music by a regular orchestra but there is no dancing. The few places where there is, most all the pieces played are American. Italians are much better dancers than the Hollanders or Germans.

Back to our travels. As we go deeper into Italy the Fascist party becomes more evident. There are many uniforms seen and more boys marching. Hotels here are filled mostly with Americans and menus are typical not of Europe, but rather of America. Wine is never served as part of a meal here.

Tour rates for parties of eight or more are granted a 70 percent reduction on railroads. We are quartered in hotels on the American "pension rate"—meals are included at a very low rate.

There was another discovery I made: most buildings are plastered on the outside over brick to lengthen the period of their existence, which means that many of the so-called ancient buildings are reconstructed but retain their original appearance.

Monday, July 13

Arose after a very refreshing sleep during which it was necessary to use the covers. We are having absolutely perfect weather, soothing, warm sunshine, cooling shade and breezes and cool starry nights. W.B. says that he has never experienced such fine weather before.

We rode in a jig (of which there are a great number in Florence) to the Medici Chapel, a great, colorful unfinished edifice used for entombment of part of the Medici family and as a reception place for treasures. Most art here has been done by Michelangelo, whose masterpiece David (21 feet high) we also examined. It is perfect, even to the marks in the hands and neck. We also visited the Uffizi Galleries, storehouse for many of the world's masterpieces. Even such an unskilled eye as mine can see why one painting is a masterpiece.

In early days, the artists were gifted in many fields—art, sculpture, music, poetry. Practically all of the world's famous artists have done a self-portrait. We saw the works of da Vinci, Titian, Bellini, Brunelleschi, Giotto, Ghiberti and countless others. Del Sarto's Madonna group, a masterpiece, was the softest colored thing yet seen. The nudes are uniformly heavy and ill-proportioned. There are some Italian terms we learned to use:

American	Italian
ice cream	gelato
floor	primo
coffee	kaffe and also coffee
stop!	ferma!
Go ahead	avante
hot	calda
cold	freddo
what amount?	quanta costa?
hotel	albergo

On all the buildings built by Fascists, the date of erection is given as the year of the regime, for example "Ano XIII." All trains (and engines) have the Fascist symbol—a bundle of reeds and axe head. The Air Force here has blue uniforms, which actually and perfectly suggests the air. We saw preparations for and the arrival of troops that have been engaged in the Ethiopian war. The streets were bedecked with Italian flags and had green, red and white, horizontal streamers across and above the streets. The troops are young and did not march in the military order one would have expected. There was the usual clapping and throwing of flowers but nothing approximating an ovation. People here are uniformly against England's stand and firmly believe that "the sun has set."

There were some peculiar arrangements in this Florence hotel, the Anglo-American. Leave the key on a silver hook outside your door when not in your room!

Visited today the Pitti Palace galleries and was greatly moved in the presence of many masterpieces.

To cogitate on the fact that a piece of canvas with dreamlike interpretations painted thereon are in some cases 600 and 800 years old is very moving. The Madonna on the Chair is painted on the top of a barrel. The Royal chambers of the King of Italy were also located in this gallery. The family still uses a wing of this building in Florence. The churches here are really exhibition places, practically all of them being places of rest for the dead greats. All contain paintings and statues not directly related to religion. Michelangelo is buried in Santa Croce Church as is Galileo and Dante (who gave Italy its language).

The bronze doors of Ghiberti (which Michelangelo termed fit to be the "Doors of Paradise") are perfectly astounding. They are tied into a

The Doors of Paradise,
Lorenzo Ghiberti's bronze
masterpiece
(and detail)

number of panels, all of which are separated by richly carved channels. At the intersection of these separating channels are carved heads of biblical figures. The panels are deep and so perfectly done that one imagines they are photographs. There are people shown in all postures and poses. Animals perfectly formed and proportioned, mountains, trees, houses, temple designs, sky scenes.

I went tonight in a cab with W.B. to the mountain town of Fiesole, overlooking Florence. From its heights we viewed the sparkling expanse of this ancient city. The road up is a typical mountain road, often cramped between walls of gardens or houses. The angle atop of the city is such that it seemed that the stars and city lights melted into each other. We sampled some splendid wine from the monastery—moscato.

Tuesday, July 14

Breakfasted alone at 8:00—the rest of the hotel guests still in bed. Out on the streets shortly after to get last view of Florence or Firenze and to hunt for an English-speaking barber and to buy another journal—this one being perilously near its end. While trying to find a stationery shop I noted that the traffic cops can regulate lights by plugging into a socket in the corner of the building or elsewhere using a hand switch. They are dressed in white from shoes to typical helmet. Everyone you talk with here expresses a strong desire to go to America, but they are forbidden to leave the country except for short sojourns in Germany and vice versa.

Couldn't resist stopping again before Ghiberti's bronze doors, all covered with dust. The figures seem actually alive, speaking their pronounced convictions.

Off after lunch to Rome!

CHAPTER 10

A Roman Holiday—in, around, and under Rome, and a Papal audience

Although the train is divided into first and third class sections, the passageway is free to all and passengers from all classes keep passing to and fro. The train, as usual, is full of soldiers who invariably feast their eyes on every available female. The intensity of their stares and the confidence that they'll be welcomed is noticeable to all.

We arrived in Rome and noted the large crowd milling about the station to see the Royal Family entrain for its summer estate. Surprising to me, Rome is a vibrant, alert, modern big city. Streetcars, buses and cabs are just as insistent in regard to speed, parking rights, etc. as elsewhere. A mental impression of it before seeing it was totally different. Couldn't see it as a practical, every day city, but rather one saturated with age and quietude that tolerated a lack of modern departure conveniences.

Despite its modernness with its drivers, parks, the sidewalk cafés, dance places and all, it exudes the atmosphere of the past. St. Peter's, the Colosseum, the Forum and other monuments remain as perfect representations of what transpired centuries ago. In the immense public squares it is possible, by meditating, to envision gatherings of nobles, soldiers, rulers and the common herd visiting

The Colosseum in the center of Rome

and participating in lavishly decorated functions. The strength and dominance of the various characters of history seems yet to live in the majesty of their works, which still remain.

The Pantheon (meaning "all Gods") is an immense church, the top of which is open to the sky for the intended worship of the Gods in heaven. On its marble floor are small holes here and there for drainage when it rains. Its ancient walls and court ways provide the rendezvous for hundreds of cats who somehow remain alive on the food thrown to them by passersby.

St. Peter's, the most beautiful of all the churches, is not hoary with age. Inside it seems fresh, attractive and clean. While there I noticed high up in the dome, beautifully rendered by Michelangelo, a tiny speck of a man swinging about on a rope seat, while wielding a large brush, dusting off the walls, corners and such.

There is a group of workers whose whole job it is to keep the Vatican and St. Peter's in good condition. The group has been in existence for 400 years. Present members were replacing floor marble during my visit.

St. Peter is buried in a 300-ton lead casket surmounted by a 75-pound gold cross. The crypt is below the surface of the floor and has a chapel where Masses are said. Outside is a beautifully carved railing around which burn a great number of candles in gold holders.

The main altar, where the Pope celebrates Mass, stands with both sides open and is very plain, although an immense black and gold canopy towers far above it on huge round, carved pillars.

When the Pope says Mass he faces the congregation, his head and upper torso being visible. No funeral Masses can be said in St. Peter's, save that of the Pope. On both sides are numerous chapels where Mass can be celebrated. Each has some significance, frequently being the tomb of some apostle or saint. In order to reach the top of the dome one must take an elevator to the roof and then walk up two separate flights, one to each of the two promenades. The Vatican buildings are connected with St. Peter's and the whole plant is walled for blocks around. Vatican gardens, galleries and museums are among the world's finest. I traversed several long hallways where books on early medicine and surgery are kept.

On the invitation of Monsignor Winter Baumgarten, I trooped over the hills surrounding Rome in the dark of night. It is a peculiar sensation to be standing on Mother Earth and gazing down on the sights of Ancient Rome.

Through the same gentleman, I had arranged for a trip to Castel Gandolfo to see Pius XI. After leaving the train and trudging up the paths leading to the Castle, seeing scores of cars filled with people hurrying to the same spot, one gets the thrilling impression of the might and glory of the Pope. To see hundreds of people standing patiently in the courtyard inside the walls of the Castle and to hear the quiet crunching of cars on the gravel as they stop and deliver passengers is a highly unusual experience and one not to be forgotten.

Even the guards outside and within the walls are dressed in dark blue uniforms with a broad red band down the seams, silver epaulets and cocked hats, with a red feather in front. They have a quiet but firm dignity indicative of their conviction of the importance of their office of protecting the leader of Christianity. Though the audience was scheduled for 11:30, the officials apparently were content to wait for all scheduled to appear. So, though the courtyard was packed, more and more cars continued to add to the throng. At length a large group of priests and nuns were permitted to fill up a long, wide, cool stairway. After the last of their number had ascended, laypersons were permitted to start filing in.

Fortunately, I was near the entrance and was among the first 50. When I reached the reception chamber the priests and nuns who had preceded us were found lined up in about 8 or ten lines across the hall facing the red and gold throne where the Pope stands while giving the blessing. This meant that I would be far back and would catch only a sketchy view of the Pope and other dignitaries during the ceremony. But, fortunately, the good Monsignor, who apparently has much prestige in Vatican circles, had given me a few golden words that would elevate me to the only choice position in that huge gathering of over 500 persons. He instructed me, when once within the hall, to approach a gentleman in a red silk knee-panted uniform and to request to be lead into the presence of "Cavalyare Fa-jani."

When I did so he bowed courteously and I was led past the throng through the group of protecting Swiss Guards and into an inner chamber. There I was greeted by a sleek, suave, soft-spoken gentleman in morning clothes. I inquired "Cavalyare Fa-jani? He

Pope Pius XI

nodded and I said "complimente Monsignor Winter Baumgarten."
He smiled quizzically and said to the fellow in red: "primo positi-
one" (first position). Beckoning me to follow, he led the way back

to the hall, which was now packed, with people even standing on the window sills. To my surprise, he crossed in front of the throne and came to a halt beside the Swiss Guard who was standing on the inner circle of protecting guards.

Bowing, he took his departure and I was left standing in the only open place with all the priests, nuns and people in back of me. This singular honor highlighted the anticipation of the ceremonies and my unobstructed view of the Pope. Although it was some time before the guards became rigid, indicating the presence of the Pope in the chamber I had just left, I fully enjoyed the delay from my perfect vantage point.

Finally, the guards took their appointed positions and a deep anticipatory silence reigned. The doors on the side of the throne opened and two knee-breeched men filed out and stood on either side of the throne in front. Two purple-robed Archbishops followed them, knelt on the throne on either side and directly below the throne.

The Pope then proceeded, surrounded by four guards dressed in uniforms of light and dark blue, with helmets of shiny black surmounted by a flaring gold brush effect. The Pope was attired in white, the gold crucifix suspended from his neck by a white silk cord, and he was wearing red soft slippers. He ascended the throne and stood quietly contemplating the huge throng before him. His hair, which was covered with a white skullcap, was sparse but did not seem very gray. He is short and stocky with a rather firm bearing. He looked rather pale and aged but not infirm. True to his exalted position he was of very serious and earnest mien.

At length he made the sign of the cross and intoned the Papal blessing and with a slight scuffling sound the assemblage somehow found space to fall to its knees. The next blessing was for the religious articles, many of which filled the hands and arms of the faithful.

The blessings were spoken in a quiet but clear Latin tongue. The purpose of the audience over, the Pope descended to the floor before the throne. As he halted on the last step, some sobs, a few "vive la Papa," and a bit of applause was heard. He seemed rather surprised at this and raised both hands as in a gesture of salute or of quiet. It was difficult to determine which, possibly it was yet another and final blessing. Immediately the blue honor guard formed around him and he slowly entered the covered inner chambers.

My eyes were fixed on him every step of the way and recorded a lasting personal impression. Here was Christ's Vicar on earth, the successor to both the Lord and St. Peter, in my presence. A man to whom the entire world willingly gives its adherence; the number one citizen; the number one citizen of the world; the person against whom kings, presidents and dictators fade by comparison. The rumors of his various illnesses made the imminence of his death seem real and the rather worried look he had made me feel that he too recognized that before long St. Peter's would be filled to over-flowing with those mourning his passing. *[Editor's Note: In fact, Pope Pius XI died three years later in 1939.]*

My thoughts turned to his own possible thoughts of his prox-imity to the Almighty and the prospects of his eternal reward. In short, he seemed half God and half man, merely awaiting the Divine Summons. With the closing of the ponderous doors behind him the crowd began filing downstairs and into the courtyard. With many, there seemed to be a reluctance to leave the scene, an insistence upon remaining to absorb all the feeling and significance of what had transpired.

The picture of the Pope bestowing the blessing remained with me, particularly the impressions created in evidencing that the whole honor for it was due him, that he was but an instrument through which the power of the Lord evidenced itself on earth. The picture of his departure also recurred to me with much force as I realized that I should probably never see him again, save for the pictures that would be front page all over the world at the time of his death. These thoughts remained with me for several hours. They were heightened when the eccentric Padre casually mentioned that in his opinion Cardinal Federico Tedeschini would be Pius's successor.

[Editor's Note: As it turned out, Cardinal Tedeschini did not succeed Pius XI. His successor was Cardinal Eugenio Pacelli, who took the name Pope Pius XII and became very controversial with his dealings with Nazi Germany.]

Underground Rome is honeycombed with catacombs. Under several churches are myriads of crudely cut tunnels in which the saints and faithful lived, worshiped and hid from their enemies. I visited the Chapel of St. Sebastian under which Saint Peter and Paul were buried until exhumed and transferred to the Vatican's St. Peter's. Holding a small, lighted candle, I trudged with many in uncertain steps through the passages of the martyrs. The cool, moist air seemed as of another world as it met us at each rough turn. Though I was following a party, I could not refrain from leaving the regular passageways and turning into other, darker, untraveled passages.

At one place I found the skulls and larger body bones of several of the ancient faithful. As I felt one in my hands I could not but speculate as to the presence of the soul or of the picture existence of the fellows in the hereafter. It is almost impossible to chart the characteristics of the various churches. Like the Forum, many of them antedate Christian history. They are of all ages and represent all types of architecture. Most of them have wonderful mosaic designs instead of paintings that illustrate pictorially their holy history. One church (St. Mary of the Stairs) has a holy staircase containing 97 steps up, which the faithful pray their way on their knees.

Saint Paul's Outside the Walls features beautiful 40-foot solid marble pillars. On the Appian Way is the church of Quo Vadis

Basilica of Saint Paul Outside the Walls

(wither went thou), the site at which the vision of Christ is said to have presented itself to St. Peter. Christ is alleged to have said to Peter "I go to Rome to be crucified a second time." The print of the Lord's feet are preserved in a chapel in St. Sebastian's. None of the churches have regular seats. A few benches or chairs may occasionally be seen, but never any regular pews.

My great love for mythology was treated splendidly when I took a trip to Lake Nemi, the scene of Love's (or Theus') Goddess Diana's temple ruins and of the famed treasured galleons of Caligula. The lake, as is true of so many of the small lakes here, was once the crater of a volcano. Several attempts over a thousand-year period were made to raise these boats, which were used by Caligula, not for boating, because the lake is too small, but for Bacchanalian revels. It is said that he ordered them sunk while hundreds of Romans were reveling aboard out of sheer fiendish satanic pleasure.

The Fascist regime spent many months using scores of huge pumps to drain the lake. They succeeded and at last the ill-fated boats of pleasure were raised.

All of the treasures and precious metals and stones have been removed and preserved in the national museum. But the galleons, two immense flat tubs of charred ruin, are resting in an uncompleted museum building by the side of the lake. Diana's Temple, its gray stones crumbled to the ground, rests in a clump of trees on the side of the hill surrounding the lake.

On this trip one rides for miles beside the old Roman aqueducts, which seem to be one continuous archway. Vines and grass flourish over them now as they stand a brownish ruin. At Tivoli, outside Rome, is the formal Garden of Villa d'Este. Here, terraced for over 200 feet, one sees a garden spectacle of world renown.

The terraced garden at Villa d'Este

Starting from the balcony of the Palace you can ascend by stair-less passages between beautifully shaped bushes and trees. Everywhere there are fountains and springs of all sizes and shapes. Far below the palace is the very center of the garden. One can look upon the palace between a perfect avenue of trees and see differently designed fountains in each raised terrace—all centered with the balcony of the Palace. In the other direction also lagoons, square shaped, leading up to another symmetrical rise and culminating in a huge fan-shaped fountain in front of the chapel.

The whole of this place is surrounded by the wall, which was built to protect the princes who lived there as early as 1500. At any point along the wall one can see for miles around the countryside now com-pletely covered with grapevines.

I attended a concert one night in surroundings that only Rome could provide. In the open space, provided by the floor of a church, was a space reserved for an audience of 6,000 or 8,000. In front of the audience, towering high above, were the remains of the three frontals of a church created in 57 B.C., thought to be the mausoleum of the family of Augustus.

Beneath the middle one with a temporary plaster-sounding shell over it sat the 50-piece orchestra. At various places in the audience space rested pieces of the walls and ceiling, which had, in centuries past, crumbled and fallen. At the end of the audience space is an iron fence separating it from a valley containing other ruins. At the bow of the hill on the other side of the valley rests a beautiful modern villa whose lights twinkled in the darkness to lend even more atmosphere. The orchestra is paid by Il Duce, and the 3 Lira fee is used for charity. The floor is of gravel and the seats like our park benches. It is remarkable how quiet this vast throng is under the spell of the superb music. They object to scuffing of the feet, talking, lighting matches or restlessness.

Sunday in Rome would mean only one thing—a visit again to St. Peter's. I noticed and was thrilled again at the statues of Christ and the Apostles lining the top of the facade. Below, in a square section, is a block of marble fitted into the front wall depicting Christ handing the keys to Saint Peter.

Inside were at least 1,000 people milling about in ceaseless wonder. Masses were being said in several chapels along both sides and the sound of an organ and choir in this holy of holies was truly heavenly. I descended to the passageways and visited the tombs of many of the Popes, several of whose tombs were covered with fresh flowers. Leo XIII is still revered as one of the truly great Popes. Above, the tomb of St. Peter had its usual dense throng around it.

I descended to the cupola in the Vatican "Ascensare" and walked about the roof, getting yet another view of ancient and modern Rome.

St. Peter's Basilica in the Vatican

Inside the cupola I walked around the railing, about 230 feet above the floor and got truly dizzy. When one realizes that out in the middle of this huge dome, the artist painted masterpieces while suspended in space, the greatness of St. Peter's and its history is readily recognized.

A few observations about Roman life: Street car passengers must enter cars at the rear and get off in the front and are fined for failure to do so. Men must wear coats in streetcars—cars start by conductor's whistle, some cars are in three sections, others are two-decked like buses. Cars are prohibited from blowing horns and the pedestrian is supposed to have the right of way. The number of close calls is astounding—you must retain stubs on streetcars. Otherwise, if a Comptroller boards the car and goes around, you'll have to pay again or get off. Fare is 60 cents (4 cents American). Cars are green as are busses. Seats are poorly placed and of wood only.

Bands play practically all American tunes—the rhythm too fast but harmony good—singing is funny and terrible.

Railroad station master—"Capostazione" runs around in a long black linen coat. Signs say things like "Vistato Sputre"—no spitting and "Vistato Fumare"—no smoking, "Primo Piano"—first floor.

Most wine and dance places are outdoor gardens using unique lighting effects in the trees and bushes. Such gardens are ineffective in the U.S. except in the South due to their uncertainties and humidity even in clear weather.

Few places serve food—only gelati and drinks. The first drink costs at least 10 Lire (80 cents). (Follow ups are 40 cents.) With this, however, it has beautiful surroundings, excellent service, a band that seems to play constantly and a few dancing numbers, solo or chorus.

The name of an Italian book I saw was "The Great Pandolfo"—by W.E. Locke. [Editor's Note: This would have been significant to my father because he had a good friend in Chicago named "Joe Pandolfo."]

A delightful feature is the great willingness (or possibly obedience to man) of the Italian women to dance. In several visits I witnessed only a few rejections during several long evenings. Most of them apparently feel obliged to accept. This conduct is surprising in that rarely does the fellow invite the girl to his table or buy her a drink.

Sunday being the traditional show night I betook myself to the Casina Valadier where, surprisingly, I found the theatre to be an outdoor garden. A more atmospheric setting for opera star and actor Lawrence Tibbett's motion picture, "Metropolitan," could not be found. The movies here were divided into parts, after each of which the beautiful lights of the garden were flashed on and the audience relaxed in the flower scented air and enjoyed a cigarette. At the conclusion of the movie, a hot band was ready to play while the chairs were removed from the floor. The little table lamps under trees and vines were lit and the stage was set for an evening of drinking and dancing. After listening to some particularly hot "riffs" from this "jam" band, I decided to remain and dance with two Italian girls, both of whom were excellent dancers and reminded me of two Chicago Italians. To conclude, I ventured a swing with the "primo ballerina," a perfectly gorgeous golden blonde who spoke Italian, French and German but practically no English, so these thoughts racing through my mind did not find utterance. I was rather surprised to find that despite the artistry of her show dance that her ballroom attitude and dancing was far more biological than artistic. However, I do greatly regret that in this instance, silence was not golden.

CHAPTER 11

Genoa, Milan, and the Italian Lake District

Monday, July 20

Up at 5:45 a.m. for early departure for Genoa—here spelled Genova. The innate greatness of Rome surges upon you as you contemplate leaving her. You again feel the actual presence of the departed great of the ages.

Pisa—leaning tower—church Baptistry in a small uninteresting town. Fourteen feet out precipice lacks one foot of losing balance. Reputedly, from its top, Galileo proved the law of falling bodies. It's possible to walk inside to the top. Stairway is a flat runway.

(It is said that Michelangelo, in fits of anger, would stop his work and return to Florence and could only be persuaded to return to Rome when the Pope granted him "plenary indulgences." The great religious fervor of those greatest artists of all time is evident in their characters, which need only God to put the breath of life in them for reincarnation.)

The extent of railroad electrification in Italy is remarkable. Since leaving Austria we have traveled on electric trains only. They are uniformly speedy, comfortable and clean. Also they make few stops. This morning we left Rome at 7:40 a.m. and travelled non-stop until 11:45 a.m.

Arriving in Genoa at 4:00, the first (and properly so) view out of the station was the statue dedicated to Christopher Columbus. On its square center-part are the words "A Cristoforo Colombo La Patria" ("To Christopher Columbus, the Fatherland"). He is pictured in a tunic and wears long hair and appears quite young. In relief below is the scene of his pleading with Ferdie and Isabella, his hand resting on a table globe, and his attitude one of tense conviction. Genoa streets are about two feet wider than our sidewalks. Old-fashioned gas lamps are strung along the middle and give an eerie effect. Washing is stretched across the street from building to building. The city is built on slowly ascending heights from the waterfront and the view from one of these lower very narrow streets is one that emphasizes the difference in altitude of the various sections.

This morning I visited the great Italian ocean greyhound *SS Conte di Savoia,* a beautiful, sleek monster resting at its home pier. It is well over the length of a long city block. Preparing to sail it was a scene of intense activity. Men on rafts painting the already white water line even whiter; the longshoremen loading large wicker baskets to the full to be derricked aloft and stored in the hold; stewards busy cleaning porthole windows and shining metal; trucks loaded with luscious fruits driving up the dock level, their loads stored aboard; signal bells being tested, the huge FASCISTI symbol in front of the bridge being polished. Altogether a revealing experience.

Later I rode out to the Campo Santo, probably the world's most unusual cemetery. Here poor families can rent graves for any period of time, until they can afford perpetual retention and receive ashes. The wealthier families have huge marble mausoleums, some actually having a church on a plot of ground 20x20. Others have huge bits of statuary in front of the wall crypt. Practically all are realistically symbolic. I even found one with a figure of the Grim Reaper skeleton revealed as a corpse, with an angel representative of the promise of life thereafter standing over him triumphantly, a kneeling sailor letting down an anchor denoting the end of the last voyage; a small boat with an angel-sailor fixing the sails for the trip to the great beyond; several full-sized representations of the rocks asunder and Savior standing before the grave; Death pictured on a racing steed lashing out with a scythe; the baby of the family being held by the Mother to kiss the departed Father; in many instances the bust of the entire family; representations of the Ascension and reception into heaven.

A famous statue of a poor woman, who had for many years sold rings of bread and saved every penny to have a grave there, is at the entrance of the cemetery. She is pictured just as she was, with hoop skirt, lace blouse, and bandanna head dress. On one arm she carries the rings of bread and in both hands a rosary.

In long hallways, stored from floor to ceiling, are the tombs of thousands of deceased. On every grave and tombstone are countless vases of flowers, always fresh; in every case even with the outdoor graves, burns a vigil lamp. The cemetery is terraced and thus provides an easy opportunity to gaze at various sized and valued mausoleums at a glance. There is a church in the center, midway up the higher terraces, which affords a sanctified place for the remembrance of the faithful deceased.

House where Columbus lived in Genoa

The home of Christopher Columbus is a tiny one-room affair closely crowded by many others. It has a fence surrounding it and an ancient tower entrance looks down upon it. An inscription on the front of the building tells of the significance of Columbus. The front and sides are covered with clinging vines. The place is really a monument, since no one is permitted inside the gates.

This p.m. another delightful train ride in the empty, red plush "Primo Classe" section to Milano. En route we "tunneled the Alps" and had a fine view of the Mediterranean and the Italian Riviera.

Milan is a large, bustling city of over a million. The focal point is, of course, the Cathedral. It is a gothic creation with Romanesque facade and is a rare beauty. Begun in 1307 it is still unfinished. Within it is very dark and smells of the ages. Its altar is elevated two levels and is located farther back after the American fashion. The altar space is so large, however, that with this elevation it seems from the floor to be a huge stage. It contains the first fully stained glass window I've seen in Italy. It is said that 35,000 people can easily be accommodated at once.

The Gothic Milan Cathedral

In a crypt below is open to view what is ostensibly the skeleton remains of St. Charles of Borromeo dressed in his ecclesiastical habit.

We went later to Santa Maria delle Gracie, the scene of Leonardo da Vinci's masterpiece "The Last Supper." It is painted on the rear wall of the refectory and is much faded by time. It is said to have been desecrated by Napoleon's soldiers who used it in an idle moment for target practice. It is slightly disfigured through having had it done, but a door was cut through in the lower foreground.

Mural of "The Last Supper" by Leonardo da Vinci

Milan has streetcars operating on the same plan as the streamlined cars of Wentworth Avenue in Chicago. Standing in the front gardens of the Savoia while the ensemble played romantic airs was a stimulating experience. How easy it is to become a member of the upper strata if one has sufficient money! Attachés of hotels throughout Europe are most pronounced in their recognition of the upper class. To be more than civil to them results in their loss of respect for you.

The guide we had in Milan had to speak English, French, German, and Italian for the various persons on the tour.

Wednesday, July 22

We departed at 2:00 for Como in the famed Italian lake district. A two-hour boat ride, during which the much talked about villas were much in evidence with beautiful hills providing the background, was cool and refreshing. Italy, as it comes North, becomes less Italian and more French and German. The hotel, a very comfortable and homey one, had few guests and that fact and the very solicitous service heightened the impressions of the rarity of this feeling. This coming under a brilliant moon and very twinkling stars, I spent much time on my balcony.

Lake Como in northern Italy

from **Childe Harold's Pilgrimage by Lord Byron**
" . . . Fair Italy!
Thou art the garden of the world, the home
Of all Art yields, and Nature can decree,
Even in thy desert, what is like to thee?
Thy very weeds are beautiful, thy waste
More rich than other climes fertility;

Thy wreck a glory, and thy ruin graced
With an immaculate charm which cannot be defaced."

The Hotels we stayed in:

City	Hotel Name
Rome	Flora*
Genoa	Savoia—Majestic
Milan	Principe di Savoia
Menaggio	Grand
Lucerne	Palace
Interlaken	Eden
Paris	Bochy-Lafayette
London	Bonnington

*[Editor's Note: *The Flora on Via Venetta is now a Marriott where we stayed during visits in 2000 and 2007.]*

Poem by nameless person

"Oh land of beauty, garlanded with pine,
luscious grape vines beneath whose vaulted
skies of blue eternal marble mansions rise,
and create flowers from every lattice line
Still have the nations striven of yore
For thy fair fields lovely as Eden's plains;
Thy temples and thy cities by the main
Throned roar and gray upon the rocky shore
Who hath seen thee—Is never in his heart
The heart grows wholly old! some youthful zest
of life still lingers some bright memories

And when the nightingales in autumn chill

Fly forth, a yearning stirs his spirit still

to fly with them toward sunny Italy!"

The hills across the bay, so solid during the day, become at night a string of pearls, with their bright jewels on the upper reaches. It would seem that these experiences are very properly limited in frequency because otherwise the sensation would become dull.

Thursday, July 23

I awakened at 7:00 a.m. with the two big tall doors in my room wide open and the sun already high in the heavens and warm in its intensity. The pleasantness of the breeze from the bay passing over the flower scented garden below made those lolling moments ahead highly delectable—to which W.B. would resound—Rrright!

Nothing seems quite so completely comfortable as lolling about in the lounges of luxurious hotels during idle mornings; or strolling in delicately scented gardens beside a quietly stirring lake with green carpeted hills tufted with snow on their peaks easing the eye at a distance. Such experiences and their resulting reactions enables the traveler to pacify his recognition of the ever necessity of movement. They were a quieting boon effectively balancing the hurried nature of the European tourist.

This afternoon went swimming at another Lido with three of the girls. The place was designed and built at a bend in Lake Como by Fascisti youth. It has a small but beautifully modernistic dining room.

It is so designed that its circular front enables practically all tables to face on the lake scene. Instead of walking out in sand and gravel to a satisfactory plunging depth as our beaches require, this is designed with wide concrete steps down, which you walk to the proper depth. We rested on golden sand in a dazzling sun with rolling green hills capped with snow surrounding you, which is rather a thing to notice and feel. Ordering a Frappé Lido served on the terrace I was surprised and delighted to find it a duplicate of our own luscious pineapple milkshakes. This being our last night in Italy, W.B. and I killed a bottle of choice Moscato. Tip for future use: This is a delicious wine suitable for teetotalers.

Later, with a stroll along the promenade with Lucy and Bobbie, we took a craze for pastries and returned to the hotel with a large plate full of them. Sat in W.B.'s room munching them and regaling each other with mimicry and could not retire without a long sojourn on my balcony drinking in, for the last time, the heavily scented air of this typical Italian scene.

Swiss Flag fluttering over the Alps.

CHAPTER 12

The Scenic Swiss Alps

Friday, July 24

I had breakfast in the garden and bade fond farewells to the ever-solic-
itous staff before boarding a relic-mountain train to the Swiss boat.
The engine was of the shrilly-shrieking type, which occasionally had to
back up for a running start.

The boat trip was a delightful interlude to the first train ride
to Lucerne (in European spelled Luzern). It was again punctuated
with cruelly raucous but delicious laughter at the discomfiture of
an old couple's misfortune in having their bags selected for customs
inspection.

About midway on the lake to Lugano, the Swiss frontier is
reached. The tranquil impressions that the red flag with centered
white cross creates is very touching and comforting. The feeling
and the assurance that it is a nation devoted to peace captures one
completely after the meaningful military intensity of Germany and
Italy. The scene is a cleaner, neater one, people of distinctly Northern demeanor.

Had first grand coffee aboard a crack modern electrified train
and it tasted perfect despite the price of 30 cents per cup.

The climate here is refreshing and invigorating, the hotel superior in luxuriousness and service even to those of Italy. The food
savors of the German touch and is tastefully prepared. Lucerne has a

small park-like section devoted to a monument and museums. The monument is carved out of the side of a rocky hill—a fallen lion commemorating the valiant attempt of the Swiss guards to protect the Tuileries in France during the Revolution. The park has many crater-holes and boulders preserved from the glacial period.

Lucerne is a town intensively commercial, having block after block of shops, carrying high-class merchandise for tourists. The watch and jewelry shops are very modern and are simply bulging with countless hundreds of very newly designed items, which are of unusually high price. Everything about the place suggests catering to wealth. English seems to be the commonest tongue spoken. It is something of a relief to purchase something, and ask and be told exactly how much it costs. Swiss money is of high value as tourists soon discover when they obtain the three francs for one dollar. The component part of the franc is the centime (sahm-teem).

German influence is also noted in the use of the featherbed (a light bed, very warm and comfortable). Here at the magnificent Palace Hotel one cannot approach a door without having an attaché open it for him. If you read in the lounge, one of them immediately moves a lamp over behind you. If you are carrying your key around you will be saved these few steps by taking the key for you. They pay no attention to your private goings on, but stand ever ready to offer whatever service they sense you need.

Saturday, July 25

Breakfasted at huge garden promenade window and watched rain as though it were a curiosity. It is the first time since June 12 that we actually have had to remain inside. Incidentally, it is almost a pleasure to remain in surroundings such as these. The view of the mountains, lake and avenues is perfect and all around is a quietly contented attitude. To be definitely considered a person worthy, on the basis of attire and attitude, to be a guest inside such splendor is truly satisfying. There is no pomposity, artificiality or stiffness about—it is merely a recognition of what actually exists.

The churches here have two steeples inside and flaring out at the base reaching up to a very slender tip. The Swiss villa is called "Chalet." Coffee for breakfast is always accompanied by *hot* cream. Practically all sugar throughout Europe is cube. There are very few salt shakers and pepper is grated out of the bottom of the shaker by twisting the top. The fronts of railroad stations are covered with metal advertising signs. The ads in streetcars, if anyplace, are on the windows. There are none along the top molding.

A great percentage of the cars have clocks, while there are practically none in public view as for signs for stores. Conductors carry a large leather satchel out of which they make change. It is a slow and laborious method since they frequently have to dip down for several handfuls before spotting the right coins.

The recognition of the superior quality of America and Americans is very satisfying. Every foreigner *craves* the opportunity to come to the U.S.

Como Lago district is one of the most beautiful in Italy. Most of the lakes are volcanic craters with reasonable size mountains on either side covered with rich green grass and studded with beautifully shaped tamaracks, beaches, cypress and pines and the whole tufted with snow, the picture is one of sheer beauty. The blueness of the sky and the fresh greenness of the foliage give the water an iridescent effect. Colors of shimmering blue, green, topaz, turquoise, and amethyst alternate in a delicate mirror like effect. Sometimes the whole effect is like a perfectly molded, exquisitely colored bit of pottery.

Tunneling the Alps is an interesting and illuminating experience. The Alps were tunneled in 1882 and electrified trains are used

The Swiss Alps

exclusively for such passages. In fact, Switzerland's railroads are all electrified and offer superb service. One tunnel is eight miles in length. It is interesting to keep an eye on one object such as a church and to note how the train circles above and around it. The Saint Gotthard pass is the most famous. Others are the Brenner and Simplon passes. Interlaken, like Lake Lucerne, is a community entirely devoted to the tourist traffic. In both cases some of the towns are composed entirely of hotels and shops.

The Swiss are a rather enigmatic people—seemingly animated but with restraint. In this they are like the Hollanders. Both countries are on the gold standard and prices are very high so they are legitimately independent. The Swiss standard is the franc (33 cents) and the smaller combination is centimes. The Swiss are the first Europeans to serve coffee comparable to that of America. They use warm cream, whereas all others use warm milk.

While I was in Interlaken, the Swiss government issued an injunction against further mountain climbing of difficult peaks. The reason was the death of six Germans who were trying for a $30,000 prize to be bestowed at the Olympics. The Swiss are skillful but careful climbers and had discouraged the attempt.

Sunday, July 26

Due to the early trip up the mountains and little time for Mass, I had to forego religious observance of the day. We traveled by cab up the various ranges and were thrilled at tunnels, huge cracks between parts of rock, roaring powerful gushes of water, heating huge craters inside. It is similar to Niagara Falls inside near the crashing water, but more thrilling because the force of the stream (which is of melted mountain top snow) actually vibrates the perches one stands on.

It is made more chilling by fiery red electric illumination. Despite the loftiness of the Swiss Alps, various hotels are seemingly precariously perched on the very edge. So high are they that they look like tiny cardboard boxes. "Jungfrau" is the most famous peak at Interlaken. It is the highest and most beautiful. Virgin snows in enormous amounts completely cover it and provide a ghostly but fantastic appearance. Mountain streams form from Jungfrau's melting snows. The Matterhorn is also nearby.

Departure by electric train featured leaving a bag at the station by W.B. Aboard the train we met Judge Russ Hall of the Illinois Court of Appeals.

Place de la Bastille Obelisk

CHAPTER 13

Captivating, Colorful, Joyous Paris

We arrived in Paris at 9:30 p.m. Ah, captivating, colorful, joyous Paris. It is all any picture can make of it. Cabs, gendarmes, people, atmosphere—all are wondrously fabled and truly exhilarating.

Some initial observations: The Café De La Paix (in the Grand Hotel), Folies Bergeres, Arc de Triomphe, Napoleon's Tomb, Champs Elysées, Rue de Rivoli, Place Vendôme, The Louvre, Tuileries Garden, book stalls, Place de la Concorde, Obelisk, Rue Royal, Notre Dame, Abbey of St Genevieve, Sacred Heart, Eiffel Tower, Le Sphinx, Bal Tabarin, Sorbonne Girls, Nudist, Eve, Heaven and Hell. Busses, shops, floor cleaning (with lettuce leaves), Versailles, cabs, (cheap), no wrong side of the street driving, the Ritz (Brandy Alexanders). Barbers, horse meat, cigars, shoe repairs, and the Meaux. [*Editor's Note: the Meaux is a community about 20 miles from Paris.*]

To prepare a day-by-day account in Paris is not only impossible but inhuman. The kaleidoscope of events and impressions is so great as to cause one to become engulfed.

The Café De La Paix is sheltered under awnings on two sides of the Grand Hotel, which is one of the corners of the place now open. It is busy at breakfast until long after midnight. It is probably as synonymous with Paris as is the Eiffel Tower. They say that if you sit there for an hour you can see persons of all nations and practically every tongue.

Neatly black-garbed waitresses pace continuously before the patrons with razor thin sandwiches, candies, world renowned French pastries, cigarettes, etc. If a person is wanted in the lobby or on the phone, a brown and gold livery gentleman passes along front with a sign containing (on demand) the person's name and the request. To attract attention he rings a small bell on the sign.

Prices are in keeping with the importance of the place. Eighteen cents for a small glass of coffee, 24 cents for a piece of pastry, 30 cents for a small glass of wine, etc. The women who frequent it are tastefully, even lavishly attired and are, paint notwithstanding, really beautiful.

The Folies Bergeres is not taken so seriously by Parisians but is a well-staged musical comedy revue. Below the theatre are sideshows featuring sensuous dancing by nude beauties.

Upstairs, in the lobby area bar, there is a small café and some shops. The show itself has a very informal atmosphere, though not as rowdy as our burlesque. It is possible to purchase standing room or to pay $4.00

The Folies Bergeres performance theatre

for a seat. Not crowds, but rather finances dictate the standing room provisions. The review is well staged and has very beautiful settings. The singing is ordinary but the dancing excellent. The chorus girls are young, beautiful and well built. Practically all the music played by the orchestra was American.

In the neighborhood of the theatre are private nude peep shows, places for a drink and a "party" and other things connected with Paris. Inside the theatre, at the box, are well-dressed ladies. As I was leaving the theatre one of them sidled up to me, smiled so languidly that I was forced to return the smile. Her only words were "Party Monsieur?"

The Arc de Triomphe is a massive square monument erected to commemorate the victories of Napoleon. Its faces are carved with events and battle scenes and have inscribed the names of all his great associates. It is in an immense public square with heavy boulevard traffic circles all around it.

On the public walk beneath the Arc is the plaque covering the Tomb of the Unknown Soldier, at the top edge of which burns the gas "Torch of Eternal Remembrance."

The Arc is at the top of the Champs d'Elysees. This is a magnificent heavily-foliaged boulevard with mansions and beautiful gardens on either side. No one, not even Frenchmen, enters it from the Place de la Concorde without emitting a gasp of wondrous appreciation.

Napoleon's tomb is a massive marble masterpiece, which is in a lower section and can be viewed from the first floor of the church of Saint Louis who was a great Christian king of the Crusades period.

Surrounding the tombs are statutes representing fame, honor and glory, and all are women. Between the statues are flimsy battle flags representing various battles and victories. Also buried in the church is Napoleon's brother Joseph, the one-time King of Spain. Plans were made to place the body of Marshal Ferdinand Foch (French general

The Arc de Triomphe at night

and supreme commander of the Allied forces in the Great War), in the remaining chapel.

The church is a very ancient one and peculiarly has countless other faded battle flags hanging about it. While there, I viewed the marriage of one of the descendants of the Lafayette family at which the Cardinal of Paris officiated.

The Rue de Rivoli is a wide boulevard lined block after block with fine shops. Also on one side is the Palace from which Catherine dé Medici gave the signal to start the Revolution, and Tuileries Gardens.

The Place de la Concorde is really the historic and political center of Paris. In its center is a 3,000-year old Egyptian obelisk, presented to the Queen of France centuries ago. On the sidewalk section of the outer rim of the drives are large sitting statues of marble ladies representing the various sections of France. One for Alsace Lorraine was black draped from 1871 until 1918 because of its loss to Germany. Each Armistice Day now, celebrations are held before it. One side of the Place is the American Embassy erected on the spot where the guillotine put to death Marie Antoinette, King Louis, and Robespierre, among some 2,900 others.

Notre Dame Cathedral is some 600 years old and was built by priest architects. It has the most beautiful stained glass windows in

Cathedral of Notre Dame

France. They are cemented in place but were removed during the war and replaced. It's here that Napoleon was crowned emperor in a ceremony during which he impolitely grabbed the crown from the Pope's hands and placed it on himself and also his queen.

Sacred Heart is a church located on a very high elevation of the city and from its steps one can see the entire topography of Paris. It makes a perfect panoramic picture. All the color decorations of the church are done in mosaics. St. Genevieve is the patron saint of Paris because she persuaded the Germans to desist attacking in one of the wars centuries ago. Her church is over 1,000 years old and is very dark and musty.

The Eiffel Tower is about 997 feet high and is used for sightseeing, radio broadcasting and advertising. The elevators go up in three stages so you just get off at each and view Paris and its suburbs. The Citroen car has huge electric engines on its sides. The tower is over 53 years old and bankrupted Joseph Eiffel who built it for the 1889 World's Fair. It is now operated by the city and overlooks the area of the 1937 Paris Exposition. The cars operate so slowly that a trip to the top and down again takes at least an hour and one-half. The top is a really dizzying height and provides a perfect view for over 25 miles on four sides.

The outlines of the formal gardens are perfectly presented, as are the beautiful buildings, race courses and boulevards. The River Seine with its many book stalls runs along directly in front of the tower. The three floors of the tower are very large. Each has a restaurant and many booths for purchase of something.

The book stalls are remarkable stands selling old books, magazines and prints. It is said that frequently old issues, even firsts, are unearthed there. They are famous enough to merit recognition by authors and journalists.

Eiffel Tower

Paris book stalls

The Louvre is rated the greatest art gallery in the world and contains the works of over 2,000 masters. Rigid tests are required of every picture before it achieves a place. It is divided into the schools of various countries, periods, etc. and includes two of the 10 world's masterpieces: the Annunciation and the Mona Lisa. Among others are: The Gleaners, The Angelus, the Sons, and Whistler's Mother. The statuary contains the original Venus de Milo and Winged Victory of Samothrace. Some of the artists whose work appears there are Tintoretto, Botticelli, van Dyck, Hals, Rubens, Rembrandt, Michelangelo and Ingres.

There is a monument now in the center of the square of what was once the Bastille, which no longer exists. On Bastille Day people sing and dance around this monument all day and no traffic is permitted.

The Sorbonne is famous as an institution superior in the consideration of literature. It is the University of Paris, located in an oldish section and very aged buildings. It has parking and student quarters inside. A practice quite common is to have students engage a French girl to look after their quarters, and to be, in addition, their sweethearts and mistresses. Such practice seems to be recognized and accepted by all.

The Ladies of Paris, who are available for monetary adventure, are strikingly beautiful, shapely and gorgeously attired. They frequent sidewalk cafés in surprisingly large numbers and are ever the aggressors in discreet advances.

If you are not in position to watch their ever-watchful eyes they will take their mirrors and smile through them at you. They will even send over a drink if you are not in a position to get to them. Their invitation to their apartment is always predicated upon your prerogative of leaving after a drink if you so choose. It was a difficulty of the highest degree to refrain from accepting the entrancing suggestivity of these exquisite Sirens, many of whom have public manners far exceeding those of respectable ladies in America.

Le Sphinx is openly a busy but unusual sporting house. On the first floor it has a large room done in Egyptian tables and cushions on the near side of a center passage. Its lighting scheme is of the indirect subdued type and the music and records from an unseen machine play in a low pitch all sorts of tunes. About 15 girls, naked save for a flimsy scrap in the middle, dance with whoever wants to dance with them. When not dancing they sit on benches at the entrance or with some patrons or at the bar. If the slightest encouragement is given to them, their arms are about you or intently explorative.

They are firm in their communication that you never have had a party to compare with that which they will provide you. It's quite noticeable that those who did accept the suggestion to go upstairs were young people or middle-agers.

The well-known Bal Tabarin is a high-class cabaret featuring a colorful exhibition of fleshy dancing and chorus work. The numbers and scenery are both easily comparable to everything American. The girls in each case are practically nude and are of the tall, Amazon Ziegfeld types. The floor is large and the band up to the American standard.

The beds in hotel rooms in various countries differ as follows: In Germany, Austria and Switzerland they are feather covered; in Italy there are fly nets and in France and England there are cylindrical rolls and pillows.

At the bar, which runs along one side of the very large balconied room, are many ladies who slide alongside you at the slightest provocation. It doesn't have a facility for sportings, so the ladies will go with you or you with them.

They are rather high class since the room has a great entrance fee of 12 francs (75 cents). The "Nudist" and "Eve" are cabarets specializing in suggestive lewd dancing and are well patronized due to the alluring character of the names. Both, as with all other cafés, are frequented by absolutely beautiful women who are perpetually open to suggestions.

Most hotels have rates that include breakfast. You must fill out a personal data sheet on arrival and on departure.

In one of the cabaret establishments, "Heaven" and "Hell" are upstairs and down respectively. In one, angels wait upon you and in the other, devils. The places are independent of each other and their success is proof of the French opportunism as regards visitors. Another café, the name of which escapes me, is underground. It has a small wax museum of provincial characters and dress. The performers are dressed as provincials and sing native French songs. There are many ballrooms for the working class and the habitués resent intrusion by "shimmers." The underworld cafés are two flights beneath the street and are frequented by the very low lizard type.

The buses of Paris are peculiar snubbed nosed affairs, neither speedy nor comfortable. The conductor stands on an open rear platform and keeps fastening or opening a silly little chain, which is just in place when the bus is in motion. The buses have graduated fares according to distance and are divided into two classes by price. It seems most peculiar, at first, to see a bus empty in front and to be loaded down in the rear section and platform. Buses have advertisements on their windows and around the top. Paris is definitely a tourist city. It has mile after mile for shops, containing articles that are particularly suited to tourists, from the lowly trinket to very expensive originally created gowns. Practically all the employees speak English and most of the places readily cash an American traveler's check or American dollar bill.

A trip to the magnificent Louis XIV Palace at Versailles, and the large and little Trianon chateaus, should be included on every visit to Paris. It is some 15 or 20 miles from Paris and is situated in an immense park area having fantastically designed flower gardens, sharply connected hedges of all shapes, fountains (each having a special significance) and picturesque lagoons.

The Palace is a vast three-sided affair with a Mansard roof around windows (dormers) and a huge open square (cobblestone) in front. Below this square are two or three sided groups of buildings, both are large, which were used solely for stables. Napoleon converted one of them into a military school and they are now used as schools of aviation. The Palace, now used for exhibitions only, has much of the original furniture, tapestry and art treasures. All walls and ceilings are heavily carved. Each ceiling has many pictures with a special significant theme for each.

Two of the main features are The Hall of Mirrors and the private Opera House of the King. The windows of the immense hall run along the side overlooking the whole garden and lagoon scene. The ceiling above required 8 years to paint, having symbolic scenes with almost full size characters. The Opera House was constructed so the King could go directly from his chambers to his box without fear of interception. His box was a wide one in the center of what would be the first balcony. The rest of either side was occupied by lesser notables. In the small mask opening of the ceiling were places for utter nobodies who could view the performance but who could not be seen. Because Versailles is a division of the government of France, this chamber is now used for legislation and for the official election of the President.

The Trianons are three-sided one-story buildings built as woodland retreats for the Queens and mistresses of the King. There is a tiny Swiss village on the grounds, a relic of the past history of

Hall of Mirrors in the Palace of Versailles

the soldiers who protected the royalty. Swiss soldiers were, because of their physique and valor, much in demand as professional paid protectors. The monument in Lucerne is dedicated to those among them who died in pursuit of duty during the French Revolution.

I must mention a very pleasant experience that took place at 6:00 on Wednesday. W.B. and I went with the girls to the Ritz for an Alexander cocktail. The Ritz is the gathering place for Americans, Parisians and the smart French. The room is done in blue and silver and has hunting scenes above in a very colorfully modernistic manner. The service is delightfully solicitous and the cocktails superb. With them are served crisp chips, salted nuts, inviting canopies and a crisp kind of fruit coffee cake. The place and the crowd are ultra smart and the tone strikingly lofty and rare.

The French call their waiters "garcon" and the French method of floor sweeping is to spread wet lettuce leaves over the carpet before sweeping.

The cars in Paris pay no license fee, the tax on gas producing sufficient revenue for inspection purposes. No horns may be used after midnight so the lights of a car are flashed on and off for intersections and when passing. The cabs are rather modern in appearance and have a very reasonable rate. No one should miss the truly Parisian or French saveur evidenced in the attire of the gendarmes. They are a dark blue with fine silver trimming, square topped hats and very swanky capes. They always travel in twos and the squad cars are open touring models in an unidentifying black.

The climate in Paris is ideal for traveling. It is dry and cool. The atmosphere of the city is charged with the unqualified acceptance of the legitimacy of pleasant anticipation. One's business is always considered one's own and the better the time one has the more receptive the reaction. The exhilarating tone is ample evidence of the reason why, of all places in Europe, Paris is the spot everyone wants to return to again and again.

1930s Austin Landaulette London taxi cab

CHAPTER 14

London and the British Experience

London, August 1-6

The city is unbelievably large both in size and population. Most of the thoroughfares are crowded with people, but not uncomfortably. We arrive late on Friday night and I was impressed with our Bonnington Hotel. After a cursory view of the section around the hotel I felt as I had in Vancouver, depressed and uncomfortable. This is the point that everyone should know and consider: never estimate a place until you have had a night's rest and a good breakfast. The usual arrangement in all London hotels is to include breakfast in the room rate.

The meal is a rather formal affair in a well-appointed room staffed with white tied tail-coated waiters. This, despite the Bonnington's limited capacity of 250 guests. The English breakfast is a genuine relief from the continental rule of rolls and coffee. It includes breakfast food, fish, ham, bacon, kidneys, tomatoes, eggs, toast and a *pot* of coffee. After consuming a goodly amount of these victuals one is better prepared to look about before settling on his convictions concerning a city. London's autos are all right-hand drivers and therefore the driving is just the reverse of that found elsewhere.

The wrong side of the street driving is very confusing since this is the only place it is really the rule. The London cabs are very old-fashioned four cylinder cars that look something like an old buggy. They are very interesting to look at and have no real provisions for comfort.

Westminster Abbey is in the same general group of buildings as the Parliament, and is a vast edifice filled with crypts and memorials. It has buried beneath it many of England's past kings and queens, politicians, soldiers and sailors, martyrs and, in a spot segregated from the rest, "Poet's Corner." The chamber in which the Knights of the Bath meet has a delicate scroll-work ceiling which required more than 20 years to complete.

Before each knight's seat and above it hangs the shield or coat of arms of his family or district. The House of Commons and of Lords is quite like our legislative chambers, but are not quite as large and do not have benches before the places of the members. One wing of the building is given over to a men's hall, which is about 800 years old.

Marking stones on the floor tell of various historic happenings on those spots. It is the hall in which England's great are placed for public adoration. King George's remains were recently on view there. The whole group of buildings is very impressively located on the banks of the Thames, with Old Ben, the clock tower of one of the buildings soaring aloft over all of them.

There is a section in front of the Abbey's altar where a 600-year-old chair built on a rock rests when the king is officially proclaimed at the coronation.

Old Ben has a deep, authoritative tower quite in keeping with the importance of the government so close to it.

The British Museum was a surprising disappointment. It has nothing unusual it in and its displays are very limited. True, it has some fine exhibits of original manuscripts, books, china, silverware and clocks, but other museums in Europe so completely overshadow it that the conviction reaches one that it is not worth more than 30 minutes or an hour visit. The National Gallery as a treasure house for art is far superior to this museum, but again, the galleries of the continent far exceed it.

Big Ben clock tower at the Houses of Parliament

St. Paul's Cathedral is another beautiful edifice always thronged with visitors. It has splendid carvings and statuary and also served as a crypt for the departed great. It is second in length to St. Peter's and also has a dome quite similar but slightly smaller. Originally built as a Catholic church it shows evidence of Catholic decoration and some of the totally different English church style.

The world famous London Bridge has two pilot houses, one at each end, and leads to the Tower of London, which is part of the original fortifications of the city.

The castle or the fortress still retains its walls, but the moat is now a walking or riding space. The walls of the building proper are 15 feet thick and wedged into a 6-inch opening for the Norman window. It was in this place that the two boy princes were murdered and where Raleigh was imprisoned for 21 years. In the cobblestone courtyard is the spot where King Henry VIII had his victims, wives or otherwise, hanged, guillotined or shot. All the buildings

London Bridge

are dedicated to some public use, as barracks for soldiers, museum of old-fashioned guns, jewel house for the crowns, etc. The Jewel House is really worth a visit, because it is only here that one can view in close range the royal crowns and jewels.

The crown of the king has some diamonds in it interspersed with 360 rubies of beautiful hue. There is always an immense line passing before the large octagonal shaped brilliantly lighted showcase. All the crowns, swords, pendants and necklaces are there, millions of dollars worth, within 2 feet of the viewers. A rail keeps them at a distance and a wire screen covers the glass of the case.

On Monday (a bank holiday—4 per year) I viewed the change of guards at St. James Palace. They have brilliant red jackets, dark blue trousers with red stripes, and a huge tousled black headpiece. They are rigid and mechanical, walking with a slight variation of the goose step.

The new guards march with the band from nearby barracks and change flags with the group, which had been on duty the preceding 24 hours. It is a colorful show and is always given before a huge crowd.

Piccadilly Circus (Circle, because it is a round public center), is a busy business and theatrical center. During my stay there were 34 legitimate productions playing. There are 52 legitimate houses and there are times when all are operating. There are of course many "cinemas" showing U.S. movies for the most part.

Practically all big cinemas have restaurants and dance halls in connection with them. The organist and stage show are still popular as are Victrola records.

There are many theatres that show nothing but newsreels and a Mickey Mouse-type comedy. The English have a plan of theatre seating which requires much thought to understand and use. Practically all of the larger houses sell standing room and have backless benches in the rear. BODUPG represents the usual types of seats— Balcony, Orchestra, Dress Circle, Upper Circle, Pit and Gallery.

Madame Tussauds is internationally famous as a wax museum. The place is very large, several rooms and a basement chamber being required to house the models. In addition there is a tea room, dine and dance spot and theatre showing latest releases. The museum was actually started in Paris about 1790 and has continued under descendants of the originators. It features very realistic scenes of English and French history, a hall of kings and queens, a hall of great statesman and patriots, a hall of leading athletes, aviators, etc. The lower chamber is devoted to "Horrors," lifelike models of killers, death masks of persons executed, heads of persons after being guillotined, instruments of torture. In this museum is what is reputed to be the original guillotine knife that executed King Louis XVI, Marie Antoinette and Robespierre. A full-sized guillotine is displayed with a victim laid on the block and a French citizen ready to release the knife.

W.B. and I spent two very delightful nights at Frascati's and at the Holborn Restaurant, both of which top most of the places in Chicago. Both are very formal and are richly and tastefully decorated, neither giving the impression of being public. The food is superb and is served by very talented and discreet tailcoaters. Both have good orchestras playing good American dance music and supply cigars and cigarettes.

In Frascati's, which is the more lavish of the two, are pedestal baskets which have beautiful flowers and roses in a block of clear ice, which fits into the basket.

The Bonnington has no heat in the rooms save that provided by a very small fireplace. They hammer on a big flat iron when people are not prompt for meals.

The busses of London are built much like those of Chicago, but outnumber ours about 5 to 1. They take the place of streetcars. The only streetcars I saw were double decked and travel underground. The buses are literally covered with big advertisements. The conductors, as in Paris, wait until the passenger is seated either up or downstairs before going in to collect.

The trip across the English Channel from Boulogne-Sur-Mer, to Folkestone, was a thriller. Arriving by train almost at the side of the dock, we went aboard a small steamer for dinner shortly before beginning a 2½ hour trip. It was a rainy, foggy night featuring a rough sea.

It was amusing to see the members of our party try to remain seated as the ship tossed and pitched. To actually direct food to the mouth was an achievement. After two courses of the dinner had been served, the female contingent started to sicken and pale and had to be carried downstairs. Everybody, sick or well, roared their approval when the whiney, battle-axe Hewitt began her mincing step descent. Old Bulbous Hewitt remained seated, stuffing himself with utter unconcern over her difficulty. He later joined W.B. and me on the cushions and remained until the end picking his teeth. The voyage was an ace in the hole for her since her display effectively cancelled any possibility of the trip to Ireland he wanted to take.

According to W.B., the best guarantee against seasickness is lying down and it worked perfectly for me.

The English appear to me stiff, insolent, independent and sarcastic. Even the guides lack the touch necessary to get tourists interested in the Englishmen and their history. Some of the clerks and a few of the waiters were civil but most of them are far removed from those on the continent. I disliked intensely the English manner of eating, and they are all exactly alike. All used a knife and fork like mechanical instruments, holding both in their hands through the whole meal.

Their habit of piling the fork full of various parts of the meal and then wheeling their head around to meet it is the clumsiest, most ungainly action I have seen at a dining room table. When food is thin and cannot be stabbed with a fork they shovel it in with a backhand movement, being unwilling to change hand positions so as to guarantee a graceful movement without stabbing. I have termed their style "left handed face stabbing."

The day before leaving I joyfully took occasion to visit Stratford on Avon. It is a picturesque little town on the peaceful Avon River. Shakespeare's birthplace is a typical two-storied English structure of stucco and outside stained wood trimmings. The room in which he was born is a small, square low ceilinged one facing the street. It is bare now, save for his reputed school desk. In various rooms are displays of his original manuscripts, playbills in which he is listed as a leading comedian and author, and press notices as to his rise. In the rear of the home is a lovely garden and gravel path preserved in its original style. The town has a Shakespearean playhouse on the banks of the Avon in front of which is a fine statue of him surrounded on the corners of the base by leading characters of his plays.

In the nearby country is the "Collegiate Church of the Holy Trinity" where the poet, his wife and child and her husband lie buried

Shakespeare's birthplace in Stratford on Avon

just inside the altar railing. Their places are marked only by a flat undecorated piece of stone flooring with crudely carved inscriptions thereon. In a case are the pages of the church records showing the entry of his birth and death.

The cemetery surrounding the church shows many crude flat slabs as headstones, some being 1700 dates. Wife Anne Hathaway's thatched-roof cottage is a short distance away in the countryside. It was built in the 16th century and is still intact in many sections.

In the living room of the house is the seat made of flat rough boards where Shakespeare and Anne are reported to have sat beside the fireplace. He is reputed to have gone to London after having been convicted of stealing a fowl. The whole countryside seems to be alive with legends of him and to be dedicated to the pleasant task of preserving the memory of him.

Warwick is a famous English castle which today houses the family of the Earl of Warwick. It is a beautifully laid out place with rolling well-kept lawns and is surrounded by a high wall. The castle housed many of England's great rulers and has relics of old art, suits of armor, firearms, Queen Anne's stuffy bedstead, and other historical remnants.

The Venetian gardens are carefully planned and are perfectly maintained, the hedges so neatly shaped as to appear to have been poured in concrete into their shape. A great Venetian flower vase having a diameter of 10 feet and decorated with delicate carvings reposes in the middle of the greenhouse.

The English countryside is truly beautiful. Very little farming is done and this fact permits the growing of many trees and picturesque hedges to separate the fields. The great amount of greenness makes them restful looking and alluring to the traveler.

The Old Curiosity Shop, immortalized by Dickens, is a dumpy, wooden, two story structure selling print cards, plaques, and so on. It is a cozy little place with narrow stairways and is very properly located on a backstreet.

An observation: England's courtrooms are much like our own, save the witness stand, which looks like a small animal pen and the lawyers who wear short, curled gray wigs and black robes and white combination neck pieces and bibs. They speak from a row of benches about 15 feet from the judge, who is elevated on a high bench. Although the distance requires the attorneys to speak loudly, the English they speak is very difficult to understand. The English are very careful about visitors, requiring them to give all pertinent information about themselves, show their passports, declare their length of stay, time and place of departure, name of boat, and the like.

London's shops are all up to date and feature things definitely in style. I have never seen so many haberdasheries featuring fine merchandise. There are countless arcades in the buildings along the principal streets. Neon lighting makes its downtown section look busier and brighter than Broadway. I have been told that the huge number of streetwalkers was really a problem. I noted fewer than in any continental city. Its newspapers are many, but none feature headlines, and all are poor examples of typography. In some instances ads appeared on the front page.

London proved a very interesting city, both for its evidences of antiquity and for its modernity.

CHAPTER 15

Heading Home

We were all happy to climb aboard the Southampton Boat-Train Thursday afternoon, August 6. The train, which travels from London to the docks of Southampton on England's southern coast, is composed entirely of persons sailing that day. We were taken by a tender to the open bay where, after a short wait, the boat *Statendam* came into sight. She pulled alongside and we scampered over the jiggly gangplank for our last lap. The *Statendam* is the flagship of the Holland America cruise line and is a fitting ship for that honor. She is very long, large and speedy. As is true of all large, fast ships, it vibrates a bit, but is wide enough to conquer rolls and waves.

Coming off the gangplank into the ship's first-class reception hall, we were the cynosure of all eyes of those aboard. Those who were not in the reception hall were strung along the deck railing. As some friend was sighted, a delighted cry would be heard. This boarding an ocean liner far out in a bay is a rather peculiar sensation. The liner seems so huge, the ship's tender so small, and the distance down to the water so great. After going to our staterooms we prepared for dinner, which was served immediately in a mahogany paneled, indirectly lighted room. So popular is this ship that it is necessary to group diners into two divisions.

After dinner we started an inspection tour, which took us from the third-class section at the very end of the boat to the strikingly

Holland-America Line

Passenger List, Holland-America, *T.S.S. Statendam*, 6 August 1936

Cabin, Tourist and Third Class Passenger List for
the *T.S.S. Statendam* of the Holland America Line

Departing 6 August 1936 from Rotterdam to New York and Boston
via Boulogne-sur-Mer and Southampton

Commanded by Commodore J. J. Bijl

Excerpted List of Tourist Class Passengers...

41. Mrs. Susan H. Conlan	**50. Mr. Francis J. Daily**	58. Mrs. W. F. Delaney
42. Miss Edna M. Conlan	51. Mrs. Robert Daley	59. Mrs. W. C. Dooris
43. Mrs. Thos. J. Connor	52. Mr. A. S. Daniel	60. Miss M. C. Dooris
44. Miss Bertha Cook	53. Mrs. A. S. Daniel	61. Miss Eliz. Dorward
45. Miss Esther Cook	54. Mrs. Ryle Danielson	62. Mrs. Blanche Douglas
46. Mr. Sam Cooper	55. Mrs. Mary Dankwerth	63. Mr. Wm. Downing
47. Mrs. Sam Cooper	56. Mrs. W. Decker	64. Mrs. Wm. Downing
48. Miss Irene Copeland	57. Mrs. Pauline	
49. Miss Eleanor W. Crane	Dejonckeere	

Notice: All Passengers will receive a landing card and are requested to present same before leaving the steamer to a U.S. Immigrant Inspector for endorsement.

Ships List of Senior Officers and Staff

Captain: Commodore J. J. Bijl, Commander	Physician: Dr. TH. N. CASSIDY
Chief Officer: J. MUNNIK	Purser: G. V. REYNTJES
Chief Engineer: A. Van SON	Chief Steward: R. SOBERING

August 1936 Westbound Voyage—*T.S.S. Statendam*

Date of Voyage: 1936 August 6
Vessel: *Statendam*
Class: Cabin, Tourist and Third Class Passengers
Route: Netherlands to the United States via France and the United Kingdom
Ports of Call: Rotterdam » Boulogne-sur-Mer » Southampton » New York
Captain: Commodore J. J. Bijl
Transcription: Paul K. Gjenvick
Récapitulation:

Cabin Class : 380	Third Class: 219
Tourist Class: 325	Senior List of Senior Officers and Staff: 6
Tourist Class S.T.C.A. Staff: 5	Orchestra: Ohio Wesleyan Parsons

beautiful first-class section, which occupies from the prow of the boat, over half the space. In it are heavily-paneled, fire-placed studies (libraries), thick rugs, deep reclining chairs for luxury lounges, cocktail rooms, cafés, and more, all done in the very latest in decorations, furnishings and lighting. In its lower sections are the marbled Roman pool, Turkish baths, gymnasium, barbershop, tailor and laundry.

The Grand Lounge aboard the T.S.S. Statendam

The crowd seems happy to be aboard a fine ship and to be heading for home, but they also seem inactive and tired. Though there were two dances in progress only a few bothered to attend. The ship's concert orchestra plays frequently in our lounge and café. This type of music seems soothing—more adaptive to the tempo of the homeward traveler.

There has been a movie each day thus far and all are well attended. Most of the passengers seem tired and lethargic, preferring to loll about in deck chairs. There is less drinking and midnight deck walking than when coming over.

I have had a rather difficult passage due to a severe cold and muscle pains. This condition is no doubt due to the complete easing up after the very active continental program. Every member of the party has had a few bad days since coming aboard. Yesterday, with my cold somewhat better, I had a very beneficial massage, which helped me greatly. The masseur told me that this great *Statendam* spends the entire winter running from New York to the West Indies, the summer from New York to Europe and both seasons definitely dedicated to serving Americans.

America is God's country. When one sees the number of steamship lines and the huge portion of the ocean traffic devoted to serving Americans, one sees that we are the people whom the world recognizes as getting something out of life. The people of every continental country expressed very profoundly their desire to come to America. Even the officers, stewards, waiters, etc. aboard boats have assimilated popular American mannerisms—speak our manner and tone, use the same catch phrases and small talk, smoke American cigarettes and generally have the American social philosophy.

During this voyage we have had considerable fog. Ocean fog seems to lie on the surface in certain areas. Sometimes it is impossible to see 50 feet from the boat, yet overhead the sun is shining. It may require an hour to run through one bank, when all will again appear clear. Yet in a short time another fog bank will appear ahead and the same blanketing effect will ensue. The ship reduces speed only slightly and blows its deep-throated siren at regular intervals.

It is rather eerie to come on a dark, fog covered deck in the deep darkness of night, unable to see over the railing or to hear the moaning of the siren above. It is most comforting too, to have confidence in the seamanship of the officers. No one has felt the slightest fear, even though unable to sleep and tossing in their berths, hearing the siren shriek out its warning. This confidence is enhanced when, occasionally, the ships stops, apparently to further an idea of safety. A visit to the bridges, where one sees the elaborate means of detecting dangers and controlling the boat, imbues one with satisfying confidence and faith in the ship and her men.

Yet when you realize you are out in the middle of the vast ocean, utterly helpless personally, you cease to worry about possible happenings, since there is absolutely nothing you could do. The lifeboat drill takes place the second day aboard and surprisingly is taken very lightly. On this voyage only about one-half of the passengers attended. Near each group of staterooms is a floor plan of the boat showing in color the lifeboats assigned to that section. In the rooms is a colored disc with the number of the lifeboat on its face.

The passenger should go on deck and locate the position of his lifeboat, carrying with him the colored disc.

On this day, Wednesday, August 12, the Atlantic Ocean is as calm as a park lagoon. Indeed, the only evidence of motion is that provided by the swells produced by our ship plowing through.

I am unusually fortunate in being able to embark at Boston tomorrow. It will enable me to stay at the famed Parker House hotel, one of the "musts" which has consistently moved me. I have long felt a keen desire to visit the scenes of our early history and to sample the hospitality and food for which that section is lauded.

An ocean voyage has so many pleasantries, one looks forward to disembarking with some reluctance. The comfortable routine, the friendliness of fellow passengers, obvious solitude of ship's men—all make for a glowing spirit and feeling of contentment. It is definitely something one should experience.

The Farewell Dinner is a happy and regretful event. The dining room is gaily decorated and balloons are flying all around. Much singing, shouting and laughter is heard and the musicians stroll around serenading the guests.

The menu is very select and the service (always good) is better than ever on the Farewell Night. It has always been a source of pleasure for me to be able to tip in accordance with excellence of the services rendered me. The American tradition of big-hearted fairness is something to be thoroughly proud of, and the esteem in which we are held by all serving us is ample proof of our standing.

This morning, Thursday, August 13, I am up early and already packed, preparatory to disembarking in Boston. The sun is shining brightly and the New England coastline can be dimly seen in the distance.

CHAPTER 16

Home Sweet Home
—Beantown blast

I feel refreshed and exuberant when I hear a Boston station playing a Fats Waller recording of "You're Just a Fair Weather Friend." To be back again keeping time to the rhythm and tempo of America is a good feeling. I missed it greatly and now appreciate it more than ever. I know now that where we are born, live and mature is the place Nature best suited us for. It is the place of which we feel ourselves a part, where we feel happiest and most contented.

Our docking at Boston is also a "best" or "first" on trip happenings in that this is the first landing of a Holland America ship in Boston. As the ship slowly passes up the bay, we who are leaving it are inspected and our passports inspected by customs and immigration officers.

With just a moment to spare, I bid a fond farewell to W.B., a close friend for the past 61 days. His characterization of me as a delightful traveler added much to my pleasure in memory of this trip. Being unable to separate five ladies sufficiently to bequeath a few words to each, I chose a delightful alternative—kissing each a fond adieu to the applause of the interested bystanders.

After going down the gangplank, we were delayed for an hour. Hundreds of bags were sorted, lists obtained from customs officials, and bags opened and examined. At last, my bags having had a very superficial examination by a friendly, talkative officer, I cabbed it to the famed Parker House. Here I rested and gratefully smoked a cigarette enjoying the realization of another profound desire—to stop in Boston at this hotel. My letter from W.B. has obtained for me free sightseeing and I'm off this afternoon for Lexington and Concord via the route taken by Paul Revere.

I saw Beacon St.—abode of the gifted few, e.g. Oliver Wendell Holmes—(the door was open to identify it as his home).

Friday, August 14

Yesterday's trip was a splendid tonic for the re-affirmation of the glory of America and Americans. The view of the house of the departed martyrs, the meeting places, battlefields, monuments and graves is a very moving experience. The memory of them and their glorious deeds remains indeed alive in the hearts of all true Americans and their perpetuation needs only a visit to the scenes of their inception. Bunker Hill Monument rests on the prow of the hill where the battle was actually fought.

Old North Church remains just as it was, serene and dignified, apparently proud of its contribution to American freedom. Old Ironsides rests peacefully at its berth in the Charlestown Navy Yard, visited by thousands who read of its great record. Paul Revere's house remains as it was, filled with his items of need—chairs, saddle bags, and the like. His house contained some of the "defective glass" which time and the actions of its chemicals turned to a lavender stain.

Faneuil Hall's first floor is a produce market, kept so because of a provision in its deed. The second floor is the meeting hall and is still so used. Boston people like to say Boston is a place where Cabots speak to the Lowells and the Lowells speak only to God. You go upstairs to the subway and downstairs for elevated-surface of all three levels of the North Station.

The Harvard Bowl was built on the same plan and design as the Colosseum in Rome.

To happily complete my stay in Boston, I betook myself to Fenway Park to see another great American, Lefty Grove. He pitched wondrously to shut out the Senators 9 to 0. In the evening, I could not resist the desire to hear Will Osborne and his superb aggregation play at the Metropolitan Theatre. How fortunate are the Bostonians! He was to play for dancing in the theatre's Platinum Lounge where patrons may dance free of charge after the performance.

New York, 1936

CHAPTER 17

Start Spreading the News— New York, New York

Saturday, August 15

Off at 10:00 by bus for New York. Pass through all the well-known places in Massachusetts, Connecticut and eastern New York.

In Boston I saw the sign of a person named Francis Daily who was in real estate and one for a Joseph Pandalfo, a Boston tailor, same spelling as my friend in Chicago.

At New Haven we actually rode around Yale. Its building and campus impressed me far more than did Harvard's. I have now seen each of the "Big Three" and feel definitely that they have nothing on any of our great Midwest schools. Seeing the towns and cities so frequently mentioned in the press was a fortunate experience in that I now know that they are quite like all other places. Brookline, Mass., like Oak Park, IL—a rich, independent town—was not inspiring. The famed tennis courts were particularly commonplace.

Back in New York at the Wellington and greeted with rain and high humidity. Passing through the Jewish section of New York and Harlem was revealing as to the large populations of both people. Harlem will take a blow to its fame in the fall when the famous Cotton Club moves to Connie's Inn on Broadway in September.

It is difficult to continue recording impressions, and I believe I will conclude the summary of this trip now. It is well known that after a certain period one simply ceases to record impressions.

Union Stockyards Gate on the south side of Chicago

Whether that point has been reached or if it's merely the heat, I don't know. I reserved my seat in the Luxury Ltd. for Chicago tomorrow afternoon and I really do look forward to the beginning of the last lap.

THE END

Epilogue

My father returned safely to Chicago in the midst of the summer heat wave with a lifetime of memories stored in his active mind and fortified by the contemporaneous impressions he recorded in the journals he kept with him all his life and which I retrieved and treasured after his death in November, 1997, at the age of 92.

He remained in Chicago for the rest of his life and proceeded to obtain his Master's Degree in Education from DePaul University in 1938. He married my mother, Eileen (O'Toole) Daily, in December 1939, and I, their only child, was born in 1942.

He had a distinguished career in public education, serving as an English teacher and Assistant Principal in charge of Discipline, Athletics and Public Relations at Chicago Vocational School (CVS), the largest public high school in Chicago, from its opening in the 1940s until his retirement in 1964.

Regrettably he did not return to Europe or travel extensively after his marriage, but he was a voracious reader who maintained a strong and lively interest in national and international affairs, literature, drama, history and music throughout the course of his life, which he lived to the fullest.

His frequent references to his experiences and impressions on this "trip of a lifetime" underscored the importance it played in shaping and influencing his long life of humble service and his many impressive achievements, which are his lasting legacy. The detailed journals he kept have remarkable application to the events of our own day and are in the best sense a timeless tribute to my father's appreciation and celebration of a life well lived.

—*Frank Daily*

Acknowledgments

While I heard many stories about my father's famous "trip of a lifetime" throughout my childhood, I never actually saw or even knew for sure that he had written journals to record his thoughts, impressions, and descriptions of his travel, and that he had kept them with him throughout his life. Then I came across two worn and weathered journals while engaged in the arduous process of going through his belongings and personal effects after his death.

My first strong impulse was to flip through the pages and discard them, since many of the contents had faded and his writing was in places difficult to decipher. But my wife, Julie, argued forcefully that we keep them and preserve them for some future more detailed inspection, perhaps after I retired.

We brought them back to our home, where they were added to many other storage boxes of various items from him and various family members. There, Julie protected them from two different basement floods and kept them in her "protective custody." I am forever grateful to her for her advice and wise counsel that they would one day provide us with not only precious memories, but also eloquent descriptions of travel experiences at a crucial time in European history. You were so right, Julie, and all the readers of these journals are in debt to you, as am I.

Once I began my retirement, the daunting task of reading the journals and reducing them to a more readable form made it a project that was always easy to postpone. But starting in January 2015, when I took them with me to our Florida condo, I finally rose to the challenge and began dictating their contents—line by line, page by page, aided at times by a magnifying glass—on small cassettes in a hand-held recorder. I had to take frequent breaks throughout all this effort to preserve both my vision and sanity.

When I returned to my Milwaukee office periodically, I would give cassettes—filled on both sides—to my faithful, diligent and patient typist, Kathy Rodriguez, who would work on them on weekends and at night. Kathy did a marvelous job of transcribing the tapes with great skill and seemingly boundless patience, including numerous revisions and "do-overs" over the two-plus years of work on them. Thank you, Kathy, for all your hard work, patience, and cheerful encouragement.

I am also indebted to my friend, Kurt Chandler, the former editor of the popular and successful *Milwaukee Magazine*, and a superb writer in his own right, for his countless helpful suggestions, skillful editing and savvy advice on producing a book that would have been a great delight for my father.

And speaking of the final product, I am deeply grateful as well to Kate Hawley for the wonderful job she has done in designing the book and enabling me to have it printed and published.

Finally, I am forever grateful to my beloved father for sharing his eloquent, articulate descriptions of a trip that I felt I had taken many times over the years, and for giving me his love of the English language and his fascination with the magic of travel, which has enriched my life immensely.

> —*Frank Daily*
> *Milwaukee, Wisconsin*
> *2016*

Made in the USA
Middletown, DE
24 November 2017